S0-ABC-866

One Prayer at a Time

A DAY-TO-DAY PATH TO SPIRITUAL GROWTH

by Lynne Bundesen

A TOUCHSTONE BOOK
Published by Simon & Schuster

TOUCHSTONE
Rockefeller Center
1230 Avenue of the Americas
New York, NY 10020

Copyright © 1996 by Lynne Bundesen
All rights reserved, including the right of reproduction
in whole or in part in any form.

First Touchstone Edition 1998

TOUCHSTONE and colophon are registered trademarks
of Simon & Schuster Inc.

Designed by Irving Perkins Associates, Inc.

Manufactured in the United States of America

1   3   5   7   9   10   8   6   4   2

The Library of Congress has cataloged the Simon & Schuster edition as follows:
Bundesen, Lynne.
One prayer at a time : a day to day path to spiritual growth /
by Lynne Bundesen.
p.   cm.
1. Prayer.   2. Prayers   3. Devotional calendars.   I. Title.
BL560.B82   1995
291.4'3–dc20   95-37511   CIP
ISBN 0-684-81114-6
ISBN 0-684-82546-5 (Pbk)

Spiritual Narratives, The Schomburg Library of Nineteenth Century
Black Women Writers, reprinted by permission by Oxford

(continued on p.237)

One way to organize and strengthen our prayer life is to integrate our prayers with the events of daily life. As our calendar merges with our prayer, our days become clearer, healthier, more sure; others are blessed and the record of our time becomes a record of our growing understanding of prayer and the God to whom we pray. You will see as you turn the pages of this book that there is room to note your schedule as you ponder quietly a variety of time-honored prayers, prayers written in our times, meditations, questions, exercises, first-person, and author experiences. The Appendix offers biblical meditations. My hope is that you will use this book as a day-by-day guide to a year of unfolding prayer in your life, one prayer at a time.

— Lynne Bundesen

Week One

DAY ONE

There is no one who hasn't prayed at some time in some way. From a simple, "Oh God, I hope not," to the formalized prayer of denomination, to a deep, personal, silent expression to the Divine, we all pray with the hope that the Mind of the Spirit will teach us and show us the meaning of our prayers.

DAY TWO

I know, Lord, that you are all-powerful.

JOB 42:2

From one generation to another he shows mercy to those who honor him.

MARY, mother of Jesus. LUKE 1:50

DAY THREE

"I saw the river on one side of me and the Empire State Building in front of me and I said, 'Oh my God!' "

These three words were enough. The pilot of the blimp had only a few moments between the time the huge airborne craft lost power and the time it would fall into the river or hit the Empire State Building.

Rather than fall into the river or hit the skyscraper, the pilot saw, after calling on God, the large, flat roof of a nearby seven-story building. The blimp landed safely, disturbing only a few surprised sunbathers on the other side of the roof, saving not only the pilot's life but sparing the heart of the city and the waterway a monumental disaster.

DAY FOUR

The prayer "Oh my God," worked for the pilot of the blimp. Why? Because it is simple, direct and to the point? Because it is unambiguous? There is, after all, no evidence that long prayers are better than short ones, no proof that "Have-mercy-on-me-for-I-am-a-miserable-sinner-and-I-know-that-I-do-not-deserve-your-help-but-please-intervene-here-and-help-my-miserable-self" is more effective than, simply, "Oh God."

DAY FIVE

God knows exactly how to get you out of trouble. He has not forgotten how to part the sea.

DAY SIX

We may be used to lengthy prayers that sound glorious rolling off the tongue, prayers that make us look pious and sincere in front of our friends, family and neighbors, but as God is all-powerful and ever-present there is no fooling God. There is no way to tell the Divine something Divinity does not already know. We know that if prayer is insincere or recited only for effect, it is no prayer at all, no matter the length and familiarity or the text.

Did the three-word prayer of the blimp pilot work because a sincere call to God works? Or did it work because there is nothing unknown to God, no context where God is not and where someone has not been before us?

"Oh God" sums up the constants of prayer:

God is All.

Here.

Now.

DAY SEVEN

They that go down to the sea in ships, that do business in great waters; these see the works of the Lord, and his wonders in the deep. For he commandeth, and raiseth the stormy wind, which lifteth up the waves thereof. They mount up to the heaven, they go down again to the depths; their soul is melted because of trouble. They reel to and fro, and stagger like a drunken man, and are at their wit's end. Then they cry unto the Lord in their trouble, and he bringeth them out of their distresses. He maketh the storm a calm, so that the waves thereof are still. Then are they glad because they be quiet; so he bringeth them unto their desired haven. Oh that men would praise the Lord for his goodness, and for his wonderful works to the children of men!

PSALM 107:23–31

Week Two

Day One

Prayer is the language of spiritual sense.

Spiritual sense is a sixth sense. Though not as widely recognized as the five physical senses, still, spiritual sense is innate — genetically encoded in all of us. Each individual possesses spiritual sense. And as eyes speak the language of imagery, ears the language of sound, spiritual sense speaks the language of prayer. Spiritual sense is not found in formulas but in highly original and often unexpected ways.

Day Two

I will allure her, and bring her into the wilderness, and speak comfortably unto her.

HOSEA 2:14

~⁓

DAY THREE

I'd always been a good girl. I was ten when I was sent to the convent school, fifteen when I entered the novitiate and at eighteen I became a nun. I did everything I was told and was happy to serve but when I was in my middle forties and it came time to go on our annual retreat I was feeling very burdened by all the demands on me. I really dreaded another retreat where the priest would tell me to be more obedient in order to find relief from all the work I had to do. And then I was sent to a retreat where the spiritual director was a woman and not a man. Instead of telling me what to do she asked me, "What would you like to do on this retreat?" "I'd like to go to the mountains," I said. And so I did and for two weeks I just sat on the mountainside and looked at the flowers and the clouds and enjoyed the sun and the wind, and I thought, Oh God, this is so beautiful. I just lay there in the grass and the most remarkable thing happened. I heard a voice — it sounded just like my voice except it wasn't — and the voice said, "Angie, I think you should go into politics." I couldn't believe it but I was pretty excited and I ran to tell my spiritual director and she just looked at me. Well, to make a long story short I went back to my order, asked for permission to run for City Council and now I have been on the Council for twelve years.

I got that water system for the poor part of town passed the second year I was on the Council.

SISTER ANGELO

DAY FOUR

We all live in a context. The question is, what is that context? Is it theology, biology, an endless round of evil and despair, overworked lives and out-of-reach promises? Or is the context Divine — the essence of Truth. Is it what our poets, prophets and saints have told us, that "in him we live, and move, and have our being"? (PAUL: ACTS 17:28)

What context do I live in, move in and acknowledge as my individual life?

DAY FIVE

Prayer is hearing the Divine Context as if it is our own voice.

DAY SIX

One test of whether the voice you hear speaking is Spirit is to ask yourself: will others be benefited too?

No?
Yes?

~~~

DAY SEVEN

. . . [W]hat doth the Lord require of thee, but to do justly and to love mercy, and walk humbly with thy God?

MICAH 6:8

Week Three

DAY ONE

Prayer is saying *No.*

Prayer is a resounding *No* to helpless victimization anytime, anywhere.

No to fear.

No to apathy.

No to being stuck.

DAY TWO

I call heaven and earth to record this day against you, that I have set before you life and death, blessing and cursing: therefore choose life, that both thou and thy seed may live.

DEUTERONOMY 30:19

DAY THREE

It started with a pain in my leg. I limped along in that pain for a while until the day my boss told me I couldn't come back to work unless I went to the doctor. The doctor said the X rays showed I had cancer of the spine. I got my affairs in order and moved back home to die. But instead of dying conveniently I got worse and couldn't walk or eat at all. A second doctor said I might have poison chemicals in my system from the time I spent in Asia. A third doctor told me I could possibly be cured through electric shock. My family sent me to a hospice to die. Still I didn't die. A friend took me to her home to spend my last days. She pulled a chair up across the room from my bed and said, "What do you think this is? Is it cancer, is it an unknown disease, is it a broken heart or something you did in a past life?"

"It's nothing," I said. I am not sure where those words came from but that's what I said, "It's nothing."

She left the room, discouraged. I took a nap, woke an hour or so later, walked into the shower and realized I was standing for the first time in five months and that I was completely well. I went to Italy the next week for the summer. That was about twenty years ago.

DAY FOUR

Dear Miss Manners:

I agree with your theory about how to say "No." But I have tried it, and I just can't stop after that one word "No." It sounds so curt. So to cover that, I go back into all that complicated talk, and get myself right back into the trouble I am trying to avoid. Help!

Gentle Reader:

The way to say "No" is often.

MISS MANNERS

DAY FIVE

All evil strivings are directed against life. Destructiveness is the outcome of an unlived life. The evil has no independent existence of its own, it is the absence of the good, the result of the failure to realize life.

ERICH FROMM

~⌒

DAY SIX

Prayer is saying *Yes*.

   Yes to life.

   Yes to love.

   Yes to change.

   Prayer is a resounding yea! to all possible combinations of good.

   I say *Yes* to the following:

~⌒

DAY SEVEN

Just say, "Yes" or "No" — anything else you have to say comes from the Evil One.

                JESUS OF NAZARETH. MATTHEW 5:37
                The Holy Bible: Today's English Version

Week Four

DAY ONE

We pray when we love our neighbor.

～

DAY TWO

Do unto all men as you would wish to have done unto you; and reject for others what you would reject for yourselves.

Islamic Wisdom

～

DAY THREE

I work on the religion section of one of the major on-line bulletin boards. Every day before I log on I spend time in prayer. I pray to be of service, to know where to go on the board and to be there if anyone should need help. I do this as a matter of course and didn't think much about it until one night, late, just before I was getting ready to sign off it occurred to me to go look at a Faith topic I hardly ever visit. Suicide, a woman had written. Her note had been posted just a minute before, so I wrote her back immediately and told her to hang on and I called right away to the headquarters of the BB service. It was 3:45 in the morning there and they woke up the supervisor at home and he called the police in the town where the young woman lived and they went to her house and saved her. All this took about ten minutes. I was in Hawaii, the bulletin board headquarters in New York, the young woman in Oklahoma. A few hours later the young woman wrote back: "Thank you. The police were here."

Prayer works, I think, even before we know exactly where and how. All the dimensions of this event made me think how many dimensions there are to God, to prayer, to time and to space. Surely all physical barriers were nonexistent and technology was the tool for the answered prayer of the young woman and of myself. Twenty years ago I would never have thought of a computer or cyberspace. Now I wonder what the next century will be like and how much more immediate God and prayer will seem.

And now, quite a few of us write the woman regularly. She knows she has friends in cyberspace and on earth.

Day Four

There are only two duties which our Lord requires of us, namely, the love of God, and the love of our neighbour. In my opinion, the surest sign for discovery whether we observe these two duties is the love of our neighbour; since we cannot know whether we love God, though we may have strong proof of it; but this can be more easily discovered respecting the love of our neighbour. And be assured, that the further you advance in that love, the more will you advance in the love of God likewise.

SAINT TERESA OF AVILA

Day Five

Loving our neighbor as ourselves has been interpreted in and for each generation in near countless ways. I wonder myself if it isn't a life's work to know what it means to love my neighbor as myself.

Day Six

Confucius was asked: Is there one principle upon which one's whole life may proceed? His response was: Is not Reciprocity such a principle? What you do not yourself desire, do not put before others.

⌒

Day Seven

I find life an exciting business, and most exciting when it is lived for others.

HELEN KELLER

Week Five

DAY ONE

The Kaddish is an act of public praise to God. Central to Judaism, Kaddish is recited only in the presence of a minyan. The public nature of the prayer makes it one that resonates with community. The Mourner's Kaddish is recited for the first eleven months after the burial of a close relative, on the anniversary of the death and at memorial services.

Hallowed and enhanced may He be throughout the world of his own creation. May He cause His sovereignty soon to be accepted, during our life and the life of all Israel. And let us say: Amen.

May He be praised throughout all time.

Glorified and celebrated, lauded and worshipped acclaimed and honored, extolled and exalted may the Holy One be, praised beyond all song and psalm, beyond all tributes which mortals can utter. And let us say: Amen.

Let there be abundant peace from Heaven, with life's goodness for us and for all the people Israel. And let us say: Amen.

He who brings peace to His universe will bring peace to us and to all the people Israel. And let us say: Amen.

SIDDUR SIM SHALOM

DAY TWO

Rising in the morning, we acknowledge God's presence and compassion. I am grateful to You, living, enduring King, for restoring my soul to me in compassion. You are faithful beyond measure.

SIDDUR SIM SHALOM

DAY THREE

God spoke all these words, saying:
I the Lord am your God who brought you out of the land of Egypt, the house of bondage: You shall have no other gods besides Me.
You shall not make for yourself a sculptured image, or any likeness of what is in the heavens above, or on the earth below, or in the waters under the earth. You shall not bow down to them or serve

them. For I the Lord your God am an impassioned God, visiting the guilt of the parents upon the children, upon the third and upon the fourth generations of those who reject Me, but showing kindness to the thousandth generation of those who love Me and keep My commandments.

You shall not swear falsely by the name of the Lord your God; for the Lord will not clear one who swears falsely by His name.

Remember the sabbath day and keep it holy. Six days you shall labor and do all your work, but the seventh day is a sabbath of the Lord your God: you shall not do any work — you, your son or daughter, your male or female slave, or your cattle, or the stranger who is within your settlements. For in six days the Lord made heaven and earth and sea, and all that is in them, and He rested on the seventh day; therefore the Lord blessed the sabbath day and hallowed it.

Honor your father and your mother, that you may long endure on the land that the Lord your God is assigning to you.

You shall not murder.

You shall not commit adultery.

You shall not steal.

You shall not bear false witness against your neighbor.

You shall not covet your neighbor's house: you shall not covet your neighbor's wife, or his male or female slave, or his ox or his ass, or anything that is your neighbor's.

THE TEN COMMANDMENTS. EXODUS 20:1–14
Tanakh — The Holy Scriptures

DAY FOUR

"To walk in all His ways" (Deuteronomy 11:22). These are the ways of the Holy One: "gracious and compassionate, abounding in kindness and faithfulness, assuring love for a thousand generations, forgiving iniquity, transgression, and sin, and granting pardon . . . (Exodus 34:6). This means that just as God is gracious and compassionate you too must be gracious and compassionate. "The Lord is faithful in all his ways and loving in all his deeds" (Psalm 145:17). As the Holy One is faithful, you too must be faithful. As the Holy One is loving, you too must be loving.

SIDDUR SIM SHALOM

DAY FIVE

The Lord is my shepherd, I shall not want.
He gives me repose in green meadows.
He leads me beside the still waters to revive my
    spirit.

He guides me on the right path, for that is His
    nature.
Though I walk in the valley of the shadow of
    death,
I fear no harm, for You are with me.
Your staff and Your rod comfort me.
You prepare a banquet before me in the presence
    of my foes.
You anoint my head with oil; my cup overflows.
Surely goodness and mercy shall be my portion all
    the days of my life.
And I shall dwell in the house of the Lord forever.

SIDDUR SIM SHALOM, PSALM 23

DAY SIX

Do not disdain any person;
Do not underrate the importance of anything —
for there is no person who does not have his hour,
And there is no thing without its place in the sun.

BEN ZOMA

DAY SEVEN

Faithful are you in giving life to the dead. Praised
are You, Lord, Master of life and death.

SIDDUR SIM SHALOM

Day One

The truth of God's universality, goodness and allness is such an astounding and original thought it is hard to conceive that it could be invented. Where does my idea of God come from? How do I name God?

Day Two

What can I say to you, my God? Shall I collect together all the words that praise your holy name? Shall I give you all the names of the world, you the unnameable? Shall I call you God of my life, meaning of my existence, hallowing of my acts, my journey's end, bitterness of my bitter hours, home of my loneliness, you my most treasured happiness? Shall I say: Creator, Sustainer, Pardoner, Near One, Distant One, Incomprehensible One, God both of flowers and stars, God of the gentle wind and of terrible battles, Wisdom, Power, Loyalty and Truthfulness,

Eternity and Infinity, you the All-merciful, you the Just One, you Love itself?

KARL RAHNER

~

DAY THREE

I'd always thought of God as well, God — a male figure larger than life with a difficult personality. And that was who I prayed to when I was just beginning a life of prayer. But one hot summer night something changed that preconception. A bobcat came up to the children's plastic swimming pool in the patio. The kids were having a last dip in the pool before bed, and I thought. "Now is the time to get that gun my husband left for our protection." I thought I would just shoot the gun in the air and scare away the bobcat but instead, the gun blew up in my hand and I could see pieces of flesh and bone fly into the air almost as if in a slow-motion movie. What was my hand was now just a bloody mess of strings. Going into the house to get a rag to wrap my hand, I saw lying on the counter a book that I was just beginning to read. I flipped the book open and saw the words of an article written by Mary Baker Eddy a century before, "The pent-up elements of mortal mind need no terrible detonation to free them," and I just stopped in my tracks. Maybe you had to be there but it seemed as if that statement was a clear message that this was not about a gun or a hand but about elements of thought. I wondered how it could be that messages could speak through time. The doctor came and took me to the hospital and cut away the metal pieces of the gun and wrapped my hand. "You will have to have this hand reconstructed by the surgeon tomorrow," he said. But I went home with the bandage on and went to bed and woke in the morning, took the bandage off and my hand was completely normal. I began to think of God, not as a large male, but as physics itself, spiritual physics, elements of true memory and creativity and, of course, as the ultimate surgeon.

DAY FOUR

To GOD belong the most beautiful names; call upon Him therewith, and disregard those who distort his name . . .

KORAN 7:180

Ninety-nine Names of God specifically stated or derived from the Koran: The First, The Last, The One, The Originator, The Producer, The Beneficent, The Seeing, The Expander, The Inner, The Raiser, The Enduring, The Relenting, The Irresistible, The Majestic, The Gatherer, The Accounter, The Guardian, The Truth, The Wise, The Judge, The Kindly, The

Praiseworthy, The Living, The Well-Informed, The Abaser, The Creator, Full of Majesty and Generosity, The Gentle, The Merciful, The Compassionate, The Provider, The Guide, The Exalter, The Vigilant, The Peace, The Hearer, The Grateful, The Witness, The Forebearing, The Eternal, The Afflicter, The Outer, The Just, The Mighty/The Precious, The Great, The Pardoner, The Knowing, The High One, The Forgiver, The Forgiving, The Rich, The Opener, The Seizer, The Capable, The Holy, The Victorious, The Strong, The Self-Subsistent, The Great, The Magnanimous/Generous/Noble, The Gracious, The Deferrer, The Believer, The Self-Exalted, The Superb, The Firm, The Founder, The Responsive, The Glorious, The Counter, The Giver of Life, The Abaser, The Separator, The Shaper, The Restorer, The Honorer, The Giver, The Enricher, The Maintainer/Determiner, The Prevailer, The Bringer Forward, The Equitable, The King, Possessor of the Kingdom, The Slayer, The Avenger, The Vigilant/Guardian, The Propitious, The Helper, The Light, The Guide, The Unique, The Loving, The Inheritor, The Vast, The Steward, The Patron, The Protector, The Bestower.

⤴

DAY FIVE

My list of Names for God.

DAY SIX

In the beginning was the Word, and the Word was
with God, and the Word was God. . . . All things
were made by him; and without him was not any
thing made that was made.

JOHN 1:1, 3

DAY SEVEN

O Thou Who art the Lord of all names and the
Maker of the Heavens! I beseech thee by them Who
are the Day-Springs of Thine invisible Essence, the
Most Exalted, the All-Glorious, to make of my
prayer a fire that will burn away the veils that have
shut me out from Thy beauty, and a light that will
lead me unto the ocean of Thy Presence.

BAHA'U'LLAH

Week Seven

DAY ONE

Suppose you are in an occupation or a situation you feel sure you should be out of.

Admit the constants of prayer — God is everywhere and ever-present.

In an older view of prayer you were "stuck" and only a male God could get you out — and that only if it was His inscrutable will. Only if you had pleased Him and He heard you could you possibly hope to be delivered.

In the present understanding of prayer and God you are the delighted and unstuck image of Spirit.

DAY TWO

And God heard the voice of the lad; and the angel of God called to Hagar out of heaven, and said unto her, What aileth thee, Hagar? fear not; for God hath heard the voice of the lad where he is.

GENESIS 21:17

DAY THREE

The first prayer I remember saying was, "Now I lay me down to sleep, I pray the Lord my soul to keep, and if I die before I wake, I pray the Lord my soul to take."

Through the generations, the parents in our family smiled as their children and grandchildren recited this mantra of submission, fatalism and fear. Trained early to fear sudden death at the hands of a chimerical, unknowable, changeable God, it's a wonder any of us slept. I was a Monday's child. Fair of face, not much was expected of me, and I went through my teens in a world where prayer was in church only; read in unison from a text or, for a few brief moments, in the hush of a crowd, silently, unguided or through an intermediary, trying to connect with Him. It seemed no one trusted in their own prayer.

I was in my early twenties when I called a stranger whose prayers healed my son of asthma. The direction of the wind did not change, no medications were given, no visions were seen, there were no voices, no laying on of hands. Overnight the stranger's prayer changed my child from the listless, underweight, wrinkled, colorless, gasping-for-breath infant I put to bed to the sparkling, plump, full-of-life infant I picked up from the same bed in the morning — a gift from God and not some moment-by-moment anxiety.

What I was healed of was the subtle and lingering belief that I had been given the wrong baby from the hospital nursery; of believing the general opinion held about me — that I was too young, and had too much potential in other directions to be a mother. I was freed from my husband's persistant belief that I was not a good enough mother or woman. It hadn't occurred to me that I needed to be healed of any of those lurking doubts. Nor had it occurred to me that my child's health might depend on what was thought about me or what I thought about myself.

DAY FOUR

It's not what God knows about you that keeps your prayers from being answered. It's what you know about yourself.

GLORIA COPELAND

DAY FIVE

Spirit is not confined to a place and so reaches you where you are. And as Spirit is impartial as well as universal, no longer are prayers long petitions for the forgiveness of sin or the harboring of the lurking thought, "Well, I must have done something to deserve this unbearable situation." Prayer is God's answer to us that all is well.

⁓

DAY SIX

What are the good things about me? Meditating on the good in my life, what things come to my mind now?

⁓

DAY SEVEN

After a while, the son of the mistress of the house fell sick, and his illness grew worse, until he had no breath left in him. She said to Elijah, "What harm have I done you, O man of God, that you should come here to recall my sin and cause the death of my son?" "Give me the boy," he said to her; and taking him from her arms, he carried him to the upper chamber where he was staying, and laid him down on his own bed. . . . Then he stretched out over the child three times, and cried out to the Lord, saying, "O Lord my God, let this child's life return to his body!"

The Lord heard Elijah's plea; the child's life returned to his body, and he revived.

1 KINGS 17:17–19, 21
Tanakh — The Holy Scriptures

Week Eight

Day One

Who prays?
We all do.
If we can find the time.
If we have no other recourse.

⟡

Day Two

Heal us, Lord, and we shall be healed; save us, and we shall be saved; for it is You we praise. Send relief and healing for all our diseases, our sufferings and our wounds; for You are a merciful and faithful healer. Blessed are You Lord, who heals the sick.

SIDDUR SIM SHALOM

⟡

Day Three

I've never been so sick in all my life. For the first time in eighty years I could hardly get out of bed. I managed to reach the phone to call a neighbor for help, but she wasn't home. I called another neighbor, but no answer. Dizzy isn't the word to describe how I felt. I had this long-standing invitation extended to a friend from out of town to come over for lunch and I couldn't even stand. So I started to pray but all I could think of was a fragment of a line, "Rise in the strength of Spirit." It took me three hours to get dressed and set the table and pull a casserole out of the freezer. "Rise in the strength of Spirit," I kept saying to myself over and over while I was hanging on to the counter, trying to keep from passing out — all the while looking at the clock to see when it would be noon and my friend would arrive.

"Well, God," I said, at 11:30, "You've got thirty minutes." When the doorbell rang and my friend came in, I thought I would tell her that I was deathly ill and should cancel this lunch, but I poured her a glass of wine and a soda for myself, dreading the thought of putting anything in my stomach. I raised my glass to toast my guest and, to my shock, I drank the soda right down. I was completely healed. Completely. It was as if I had never been sick at all. It was the weirdest experience I ever had.

HELEN KNUDSON

～

Day Four

Ask, and you will receive.

Jesus. Luke 11:9

～

Day Five

Rise in the strength of Spirit to resist all that is unlike good.

Mary Baker Eddy, Science and Health with Key to the Scriptures

～

Day Six

Countless women through the ages have stamped their foot at God, informed God of what needed to be done and when, suggested to God that now would be a fine time to deliver on the promise. Is your name on that list of women who have unequivocally informed the Divine of your particular needs?

Shouldn't it be?

The top ten list of things I want from God is as follows:

———

DAY SEVEN

God is in the midst of her; she shall not be moved:
God shall help her, and that right early.

PSALM 46:5

Week Nine

Day One

Prayer removes our misconceptions about us and the universe. Strictly speaking we don't enjoy dominion, inspiration, peace, sustenance or salvation because we are Catholic or Protestant or Jew or Muslim or Hindu or Other but because in our genuine and only being we are the sons and daughters of God.

The inescapable corollary is that others, in their spiritual being, share that also.

Day Two

Turn, then, away from all that is false, turning unto Him alone; and remain conscious of Him, and be constant in prayer, and be not among those who ascribe divinity to aught beside Him.

KORAN 30:31

DAY THREE

A man and a woman were having a raging fight in the mall parking lot as my lover and I walked by. The woman was hitting the man over the head with her handbag, and he was cowering — covering his head with his hands. This was Manila and, rather than break up the fight as might happen in the West, bystanders, embarrassed by this domestic matter gone public, stood by giggling and laughing but not getting involved. My lover, Sam, went up to the people and began to pull the woman away and get tough with her, but the crowd started to get angry and advance on him so he backed away and we went into the mall. When we got inside, Sam was really upset, and almost shaking, he turned to me and said, "Why don't you use some of that fancy prayer stuff you keep talking about?" So I went back outside and stood there in the sun not too far from where the people were still fighting and about a hundred others were watching, and I said to myself something like: Male and female are created by God equally and equals are not at war with each other. God is not in this fight and neither are this man and woman and neither is this crowd and neither are Sam and I. God is in charge. And we are all Love's daughters and sons.

The woman stopped screaming and fell onto the

ground, weeping, and the man just stood there as a car drove up. In the car were the daughter and son and son-in-law of the woman. The daughter was yelling at the father, "See what happens when you take a mistress?" And then the whole story came out, that the wife had caught the husband with his mistress at the mall. And the son and son-in-law started shouting at the mother and daughter, and then I walked up to them and said to the daughter, "Take your mother home and be a mother to her." And they all looked at me and were very quiet and they put their arms around the mother and drove away. Sam was mad at me and started saying how he could have stopped the fight, and we began to snarl at each other. It was very strange. And later that day I found really compromising photos that Sam had taken on one of his recent trips, of a woman in bed with his shirt on. I never would have thought that the man and woman in the parking lot had anything to do with me. But it had everything to do with me. I began to understand that "outside" situations were also hints to "inside" situations.

Sam and I did break up. We were spared years of unhappiness.

～

DAY FOUR

When I pray for others am I, in fact, praying for myself?

～

DAY FIVE

Why, then, do you look at the speck in your brother's eye and pay no attention to the log in your own eye? How dare you say to your brother, "Please, let me take that speck out of your eye," when you have a log in your own eye? You hypocrite! Take the log out of your own eye first, and then you will be able to see and take the speck out of your brother's eye.

JESUS. MATTHEW 7:3–5
The Holy Bible: Today's English Version

～

DAY SIX

Who in my life today do I think needs prayer? And what does it have to do with me?

DAY SEVEN

The Spirit itself beareth witness with our spirit, that we are the children of God.

ROMANS 8:16

DAY ONE

The central prayer of Christianity and the prayer common to all Christians is the Lord's Prayer. It is prayed in unison in churches and by the individual believer. Sermons are preached on the Lord's Prayer, and countless commentaries on the Prayer have been written. The preamble to the Prayer as given by Jesus and recorded by Matthew is to love your enemies, to keep your religious duties out of the public eye, to not be a hypocrite and to pray privately in order to be rewarded by your Creator — who already knows everything you need.

Luke's account says:

And it came to pass, that, as he was praying in a certain place, when he ceased, one of his disciples said unto him, Lord, teach us to pray, as John also taught his disciples.

LUKE 11:1

Matthew further recounts these words of Jesus:

After this manner therefore pray ye: Our Father which art in heaven, Hallowed be thy name. Thy kingdom come. Thy will be done in earth, as it is in heaven. Give us this day our daily bread. And forgive us our debts, as we forgive our debtors. And lead us not into temptation, but deliver us from evil: For thine is the kingdom, and the power, and the glory, for ever. Amen.

MATTHEW 6:9–13

DAY TWO

I cannot say Our
   If my faith has no room for other people and
      their needs.
I cannot say Father
   If I do not demonstrate this relationship in my
      daily living.
I cannot say Who Art In Heaven
   If all my interests and pursuits are in earthly,
      material things.
I cannot say Hallowed Be Thy Name
   If I, who am called by God, am not holy.
I cannot say Thy Kingdom Come
   If I do nothing to bring about justice.
I cannot say Thy Will Be Done
   If I am unwilling to carry out God's will.
I cannot say On Earth As It Is In Heaven

Unless I am ready to give myself to God's service.

I cannot say Give Us This Day Our Daily Bread
If I ignore the needs of others.

I cannot say Forgive Us Our Debts As We Forgive Our Debtors
If I harbor a grudge against anyone.

I cannot say Lead Us Not Into Temptation
If I choose to remain in a situation in which I am likely to be tempted.

I cannot say Deliver Us From Evil
If I am unprepared to stand for the good.

I cannot say Thine Is The Kingdom
If I fear what others say and do.

I cannot say Thine Is The Power
If I do not show the power of God by loving others.

I cannot say Thine Is The Glory
If I am seeking my own glory.

I cannot say Forever
If I am anxious about my own daily affairs.

I cannot say Amen
Unless I can honestly say, "Cost what it may, this is my prayer."

Author/Source Unknown

⌒

DAY THREE

Give them through our hands
this day their daily bread,
And by our understanding love,
Give peace and joy.

MOTHER TERESA

⌒

DAY FOUR

Our Father which art in heaven,
   Our Father-Mother God, all-harmonious.
Hallowed be Thy name,
   Adorable One
Thy kingdom come.
   Thy kingdom is come; Thou art ever-present.
Thy will be done on earth, as it is in heaven
   Enable us to know — as in heaven, so on earth
      — God is omnipotent, supreme
Give us this day our daily bread;
   Give us grace for today; feed the famished affections;
And forgive us our debts, as we forgive our debt-
      ors.
   And Love is reflected in love;
And lead us not into temptation, but deliver us
      from evil;

*And God leadeth us not into temptation, but delivereth
us from sin, disease and death.*

For Thine is the kingdom, and the power, and the
glory, forever.

*For God is infinite, all-power, all Life, Truth, Love,
over all, and All.*

MARY BAKER EDDY, *Science and Health with
key to the Scriptures*

───

DAY FIVE

Our Father, who art in heaven, Hallowed be thy
Name. Thy kingdom come. Thy will be done, On
earth as it is in heaven. Give us this day our daily
bread. And forgive us our trespasses, As we forgive
those who trespass against us. And lead us not into
temptation, But deliver us from evil, Amen.

Minister: O Lord, save this woman thy servant;
Answer: Who putteth her trust in Thee.
Minister: Be thou to her a strong tower;
Answer: From the face of her enemy.
Minister: Lord, hear our prayer.
Answer: And let our cry come unto Thee.

The Book of Common Prayer (1928)
(from The Thanksgiving of Women after Child-birth)

Day Six

This, then, is how you should pray:
Our Father in heaven:
May your holy name be honored;
may your Kingdom come;
may your will be done on earth as it is in heaven.
Give us today the food we need.
Forgive us the wrongs we have done,
as we forgive the wrongs that others have done to
    us.
Do not bring us to hard testing, but keep us safe
    from the Evil One.

MATTHEW 6:9–13
The Holy Bible: Today's English Version

Day Seven

For every one that asketh receiveth; and he that
seeketh findeth; and to him that knocketh it shall be
opened.

JESUS. MATTHEW 7:8

Week
Eleven

Day One

Few things seem harder to resolve than family problems. When asked by poll takers what is the number one reason for prayer, survey statistics say that the majority of all prayers uttered, over 90 percent, are for family members.

Wisdom tells us that the most effective prayers for family members start with oneself.

Day Two

So God created man in his own image, in the image of God created he him; male and female created he them.

GENESIS 1:27

⟋⟍

DAY THREE

Eleanor was having another one of those conversations with her mother, the ones where all that's heard is the same old criticism, the same tired complaining, the same worn-out demands. She was a second away from slamming down the phone. She would deal with it later, or never, she thought, fighting back the tears. God, why does she always do this to me?

Eleanor moved the phone away from her ear and, surprisingly, heard herself saying silently, "God forgive me for thinking of my mother as anything but your child."

"Darling," said her mother on the other end of the phone, "have I said something to hurt you? Forgive me, you know I would never hurt you. I love you so much and you are such a wonderful daughter."

⟋⟍

DAY FOUR

We are never confronted by a man, woman or child who, in their spiritual selfhood, is other than God's image, expressing God's unlimited intelligence and nature.

DAY FIVE

Sister Eternal

I loved you when, as cherubs
We played in heavenly spheres.
And then as children, growing,
Sighing, singing through the years.

I love you now, as women,
We share our hopes and fears,
Our laughter and our dreaming,
Our memories, prayers and tears.

But I'll love you even deeper
When our life on earth is done
And its sorrow and its heartaches
Are the wars that we have won.

Then when we are Guardian Angels,
Reassuring those still here,
I will love you even sweeter,
Oh my gentle sister, Dear.

SHARON LAWLOR

DAY SIX

Is it only at those times we are not clear that we
ourselves are God's child that we see others as something less than God's child?

Today's prayer: I thank Spirit for being Spirit's child and living with brothers and sisters who are also Spirit's children.

～⌒

DAY SEVEN

But the wisdom that is from above is first pure, then peaceable, gentle, and easy to be intreated, full of mercy and good fruits, without partiality, and without hypocrisy.

JAMES 3:17

Week Twelve

Day One

To turn our random pleas and wishful longings into consistant and effective prayers we need to understand who and what we are praying to. Today is the day to take ten minutes, sit down and write down what God is.

Take the full ten minutes.

Day Two

Grant me, Lord, to know and understand which is first — to call on thee or to praise thee? And again, to know thee or to call on thee? For who can call on thee, not knowing thee? For he that knoweth thee may not call on thee as other than thou art. Or is it better that we call on thee that we may know thee?

SAINT AUGUSTINE

⁓

DAY THREE

In olden times, there was a needy woman. She didn't know it but her house had a cellar in which a lot of gold was stored. She was ignorant of this fact because she had lost her mother in childhood. So her life had always been poor and was never free from care. One day a neighbor told her: "There is a lot of gold in your cellar. Why don't you dig it out?" The woman was very surprised and responded: "My house doesn't have such a cellar. I don't know where it is." Her neighbor replied, "I must make allowances for your ignorance because the cellar is hidden beneath a lot of dust and dirt. But anyway, please dig and find the gold."

Then the woman vigorously removed the dust and dirt, digging deep to find the cellar according to the advice she had received. Eventually, she came to this great treasure of gold and her life became without care.

Nichikan Shonin, the Twenty-sixth High Priest, says that because the gold was there she should not have sought it in any other place. However, no matter how much knowledge she might have had of its

existence, unless she was willing to dig it out, it remained useless.

Nirvana Sutra

DAY FOUR

How do I name you,
when the words of tradition
speak of oppression,
abuse, and countless tears?
How do I name you,
when the words I seek seem strange, empty,
and without history or feeling?
How do I name you,
when you are beyond
naming, beyond knowing?
Yet name you I shall;
for you are my heart,
my life, my hope.
I shall name you
"the holy one who
hears my cry,
understands my pain,
and loves me as I am."
To you I pray and give thanks.

So be it. Amen.

VIENNA COBB ANDERSON

⌒

Day Five

The treasure that is buried within us is the knowledge that we are God's. What digging am I doing to find my spiritual treasure today?

⌒

Day Six

The wondrous voice, the voice of the one
    who attends to the cries of the world
The noble voice, the voice of the rising
    tide surpassing all the sounds of the
    world
Let our mind be attuned to that voice.

Put aside all doubt and meditate on the
    pure and holy nature of the regarder
    of the cries of the world
Because that is our reliance in situations
    of pain, distress, calamity, death.

Perfect in all merits, beholding all sentient
    beings with compassionate eyes, making the
    ocean of blessings limitless,
Before this one, we should incline.

              Buddhist Sutra

DAY SEVEN

O God, thou art my God; early will I seek thee. . . .

PSALM 63:1

Week
Thirteen

DAY ONE

But, we say to ourselves, I don't have time to pray. Where will I find the time? Finding the time to pray may seem to be a problem. There is more than one way to meet this problem head-on. One is to be radical about the clock. Schedule the time you pray, whether it's seven or eight or nine, whether it is morning or evening.

Or you can turn your daily life into a constant prayer.

DAY TWO

A human being who does not have a single hour of his own each day is no human being at all.

R. MOSHE LEIB

DAY THREE

Mrs. Brown — we have no other name for her — set down some of the basic premises of prayer when she wrote the following lines in the nineteenth century and set them to one of her favorite hymn melodies.

I love to steal awhile away
    From every cumb'ring care;
And spend the hours of setting day
    In humble, grateful prayer.

I love in solitude to shed
    The penitential tear;
And all his promises to plead,
    Where none but God is near.

I love to think of mercies past,
    And future good implore;
And all my cares and sorrows cast
    On him whom I adore.

I love by faith to take a view
    Of brighter scenes in heav'n;
The prospect doth my strength renew,
    While here by tempests driv'n.

Thus when life's toilsome day is o'er
    May its departing ray
Be calm as this impressive hour,
    And lead to endless day.

Mrs. Brown, like so many of us, wanted to get a quiet moment for herself alone with God. She thought of the good in her life, tried to forget the sorrow and disappointments, and looked beyond the dailiness for more good to come. Then she was thankful for the moment, which hinted at eternity.

A prayer like Mrs. Brown's can take place in a single, silent spontaneous moment. Perhaps it happens just before dinner is started, or when the lights are turned off for the night; perhaps when you are turning down the blankets for sleep. The words are yours but the essential thoughts are the same; only you and God, gratitude for now and for the ever to come.

Writing a prayer of your own with these same sentiments is easy to do. Take a chorus from one of your favorite songs and use your own language to write a short prayer-song of quiet gratitude to God for good received and good to come.

Sing it every evening until you tire of it. Then write another.

Day Four

Try to pray almost all the time of the day. At least pray, in your own words, as soon as you wake up, before you take a bath, after you take a bath, before you eat, before you start your work and before you go to sleep. Please do silent prayers so that you can avoid unnecessary criticism from family members and coworkers. It is not at all necessary that you attend a church or a temple or a mosque. They are just additional helps in the devotion but not a must.

ED VIS

DAY FIVE

O God, thou art my God; early will I seek thee: my soul thirsteth for thee, my flesh longeth for thee in a dry and thirsty land, where no water is.

PSALM 63:1

DAY SIX

Morning may be when we pray best. The dreams of the night dissolve in the daylight and, though still there, fade. We try to remember what they were and see what God was telling us while we slept.

Morning prayer sets the tone for our day. Praying before one walks out the door to school, to work, to buy supplies, food, should be as natural as opening and closing the door.

Morning prayer meets God's day. It's a raising of our hand during the taking of attendance. Yes, morning prayer says, yes, I am here in God's day.

DAY SEVEN

Yet the Lord will command his lovingkindness in the daytime, and in the night his song shall be with me, and my prayer unto the God of my life.

PSALM 42:8

Week Fourteen

DAY ONE

The five senses demand measure questions: How extreme is the rash? How deep is the cut? How long has the marriage been unhappy? How large is the debt?

Prayer, the language of spiritual sense, asks: How big is Truth? How long is Life? How far-reaching is Spirit? How abundant is Soul?

DAY TWO

For my thoughts are not your thoughts, neither are my ways your ways, saith the Lord. For as the heavens are higher than the earth, so are my ways higher than your ways, and my thoughts than your thoughts.

ISAIAH 55:8–9

Day Three

Not long after I moved into the house, the stove gave up. The repairman came, shook his head and gave me the news that it would cost more to fix it then buy a new one, and that stoves were no longer being made that would fit into the existing space.

I set out to find a new stove that would fit in the existing space. Tearing down a bearing wall was out of the question; my pocketbook could hardly bear the price of a new stove. Measuring tape in hand, I carefully counted off the inches and half and quarter inches available. Knowing that a fraction of an inch could be critical, I did the measuring four times on two different days with different yardsticks and tape measures. A neighbor measured too — just to make sure.

Armed with both a perky self-confidence and those accurate measurements, I found a stove within my budget at a store just two blocks away. The deliveryman pulled the old stove out, moved it aside and pushed the new one toward the throughly measured space. No way would it go in. "Two inches too wide," he said.

I spent several hours wondering what I had done wrong. Having already done everything I could do, I called my friend Wilhelmina. Widowed in her thirties, she had lived alone, self-reliant, for nearly a half century. "Well, dear," she said, "there's a hymn that says, 'Love's work and love must fit.' " I was not heartened. I didn't need a cheery mantra. I needed to get the stove in the space.

For three days I walked around the white porcelain rectangle in the midst of the kitchen. What was facing me was the argument that I was living in a three-dimensional world. I prayed. Not to make the stove fit. Not to get a new stove. I prayed to see all life in another dimension, the dimension where Love and Love's work fits. The dimension where there are no mistaken women. The dimension of spacious Spirit.

An effective prayer has results. A messenger came by later that day to deliver an envelope. "Come here," I said and pointed to the stove. "Help me push this into that space." "No problem," he said. And we pushed the stove into the empty space and it fits perfectly to this day.

⌒

DAY FOUR

Where does my life feel stuck? What can I pray about, what dimension of Spirit can I touch today that will change any feeling of being stuck for the ability to move on with other more pressing and significant concerns. How much room is there in Spirit?

∽

Day Five

Prayer is the delighted admission of dynamic facts and the recognition of them as realities.

∽

Day Six

Two active spiritual facts that I recognize today are:
1.
2.

∽

Day Seven

Eye hath not seen, nor ear heard, neither have entered into the heart of man, the things which God hath prepared for them that love him. But God hath revealed them unto us by his Spirit: for the Spirit searcheth all things, yea, the deep things of God. . . . Now we have received, not the spirit of the world, but the spirit which is of God; that we might know the things that are freely given to us of God. Which things also we speak, not in the words which man's wisdom teacheth, but which the Holy Ghost teacheth; comparing spiritual things with spiritual.

1 Corinthians 2:9–10, 12–13

Week
Fifteen

DAY ONE

Our enemies drive us to prayer. In so doing they become a path to God.

DAY TWO

Plead my cause, O Lord, with them that strive with me: fight against them that fight against me. . . . False witnesses did rise up; they laid to my charge things that I knew not. They rewarded me evil for good to the spoiling of my soul.

PSALM 35:1, 11–12

DAY THREE

There was this woman, a customer of the company I worked for, who for some reason simply hated me. I had never actually met her. In fact, as far as I know, I had only corresponded with her once and that was a pleasant exchange. But this woman had written the president of the company and my manager a ten-page letter about what a horrible person I was. I think she had confused some policy of other employees or of the company for my own personal fiats. All I know is that she began a public and private campaign to have me fired. She started circulating petitions nationwide to have me removed from my job.

Her campaign against me was truly vindictive. And then, one day, through some odd circumstance, I found out that the woman lived in the same remote small town where my daughter had just settled. I did not sleep all that night as I prayed to get rid of the fear and prayed to turn my enemy into a friend.

The next day I had to travel to an industry convention. I dropped by a workshop where I found women panelists and a roomfull of people talking about the harassment of women in this industry by men.

I was still thinking about this woman who had declared me her enemy, and after a while I raised my hand and said, "What if it is a woman harassing another woman?" There was some surprise and some conversation, and, by way of explanation, I added what my area of employment was.

Two men approached me at the convention the following day. "We heard you speak at the women's panel," one said. "And we'd like to recruit you to work for our company."

I had always heard that our enemies blessed us.

Now I could see the truth of what had before sounded like a philosophical or religious statements that had no practical application. Our enemies bless us. If the woman had not complained about me, if she had not persisted in her campaign, I would not have prayed, not have stood up to speak and not have been recruited for a position that is so much better in so many ways.

~

DAY FOUR

My God, I must admit I'm
not handling something well
　right now
What I mean is
　　there's conflict in me
Some things just don't
　match
　add up
　allow for inner peace
At best, today the
　usual joy
　seems
　　　　　　remote.

I confess that I'm
　angry

hurt
resentful
sad
    So sad, my God.
    So sad.
What doesn't match is that
    for (*fill in name*)
    I feel
        deep compassion
        tenderness
        an ache so cavernous that
        only you can fill it.
She's yours
    and I love her
    perhaps not as much as I must right now.
    But you ask no more of me in this moment.
I thank you:
    That
        I don't have to hide
        behind
    artificial feelings.
    That
        I can come to you
        just as I am
        just as I feel
    That
        you can
        restore
        all things

that are
  damaged
  broken.
Restore me.
Restore us.

REV. VIRGINIA HALL WILCOX

DAY FIVE

To love a human being means to accept him, to love him as he is. If you wait to love him till he has got rid of his faults, till he is different, you are only loving an idea. He is as he is now, and he is to be loved now as he is.

FLORENCE ALLSHORN

DAY SIX

The list of enemies who will bless me today includes:

~◦

Day Seven

Under no circumstance feel that your spirituality is superior to your neighbor's. The worst thing one can do is boast about one's devotion or one's form of worship. God, in the Bhagavad Gita, has said: "Whatever form men worship me, I make their faith steadfast in that form alone." So even the funniest forms of prayers are answered by God, if those prayers are sincere. Under no conditions condemn or ridicule others' religion or spirituality. Each person is maturing in spirituality according to his or her own style.

Ed Vis

Week
Sixteen

Day One

Gratitude is essential to prayer. When we are grateful for Life, for Love, for Truth, no matter what the circumstances, we are praying and finding our true religion.

Day Two

Prayer is religion in act; that is, prayer is real religion. Religion is nothing if it be not the vital act by which the entire mind seeks to save itself by clinging to the principle from which it draws its life. This act is prayer, by which term I understand no vain exercise of words, no mere repetition of certain sacred formulae, but the very movement itself of the soul, putting itself in a personal relation of contact with the mysterious power of which it feels the presence —it may be even before it has a name by which to call it. Wherever this interior prayer is lacking, there is no religion; wherever, on the other hand, this prayer rises and stirs the soul, even in the absence of forms or doctrines, we have living religion.

WILLIAM JAMES, *The Varieties of Religious Experience*

DAY THREE

It had gotten to the point in my marriage that I simply could not stand to be in the same room as my husband. There was simply nothing he did right and, as far as he was concerned, nothing I did right. Nothing. Things were so bad that I didn't even have the courage to leave him. We had two entirely different sets of religious beliefs. A friend of mine said, "Make a list of every single quality that he has that comes from God." I laughed. I couldn't think of one, I told her.

"Well," she said, "he's alive, isn't he? So how about starting with Life?" It took me six months to make a list of qualities that were good about my husband. It was a long list. And my husband came to me one day and asked for a divorce. It seemed such an odd answer to prayer.

Even odder is that I know several women who have made such a list. And some of them have ended up with happy marriages and some have ended up divorced. All of us think the list idea works.

BETSY J.

~

DAY FOUR

Count your blessings instead of your crosses;
Count your gains instead of your losses;
Count the joys instead of your woes;
Count your friends instead of your foes;
Count your courage instead of your fears;
Count your health instead of your wealth;
And count on God instead of yourself.

Author Unknown

~

DAY FIVE

A list of things I am grateful for today:

~

DAY SIX

If you pray earnestly to benefit others, how could your prayer go unanswered?

GOSHO ZENSHI

DAY SEVEN

If ye abide in me, and my words abide in you, ye shall ask what ye will, and it shall be done unto you.

JOHN 15:7

Week Seventeen

DAY ONE

Who prays?
You do.
If you are not distracted.

~~~

DAY TWO

You have wearied yourself in the multiplicity of your
ways, and have not said, Let us rest in peace.

ISAIAH 57:10

~~~

DAY THREE

Sometimes the only way I can pray is to focus on
one single thing. There are so many distractions, so
much noise, so many images, that I settle on washing
the dishes — even though I have a dishwasher. I
make a meditation out of doing the dishes. I start
systematically, scraping and stacking, and then I run

the water and I think about the Spirit of God moving on the face of the waters and I take all the time in the world to wash each dish or glass throughly and to rinse it clean and clear. Next I dry each one and put it away. By then, I am focused. Doing dishes is a great prayer exercise for me because I can see that there is a process at work. I didn't make the water, I didn't make the soap, but my hands did do the work and my mind was focused.

DAY FOUR

And the Lord said unto Satan, Whence comest thou? Then Satan answered the Lord, and said, From going to and fro in the earth, and from walking up and down in it.

JOB 1:7

DAY FIVE

seeking the Buddha
ten thousand pathways
which way to choose
seeking the Buddha
I find my own path
no need to choose

VANESSA COLE

~⌒~

DAY SIX

Today I focus on:

~⌒~

DAY SEVEN

Choose a day for yourself to meditate and pray: a day of mindfulness. If it is a Saturday, then Saturday must be your day, a day during which you are completely the master. While still lying in bed, begin slowly to follow your breath — slow, long and conscious breaths. Then slowly rise from bed (instead of turning out all at once as usual), nourishing mindfulness by every motion. Once up, brush your teeth, wash your face and do all your morning activities in a calm and relaxing way, each movement done in mindfulness. Measure your steps with quiet long breaths. Maintain a half smile. Spend at least half an hour taking a bath. Bathe slowly and mindfully, so that by the time you have finished, you feel light and refreshed. Afterward you might do household work, such as washing the dishes, dusting and wiping off the tables, scrubbing the kitchen floor, arranging books on their shelves. Whatever the tasks, do them slowly and with ease, in mindfulness. Don't do any task to get it over with. Resolve to do each job in a relaxed way, with all your attention. Enjoy and be one with your work. Live the actual moment. Only this actual moment is life. Start with a half day.

Week
Eighteen

DAY ONE

Prayer is a childlike thing. Simple, easy, pleasing to the nature.

~

DAY TWO

Then there arose a reasoning among them, which of them should be greatest. And Jesus, perceiving the thought of their heart, took a child, and set him by him, and said unto them, Whosever shall receive this child in my name receiveth me: and whosever shall receive me receiveth him that sent me: for he that is least among you all, the same shall be great,

LUKE 9:46–48

~

DAY THREE

In Sunday School we learn we are God's children. God is our Father and Mother and gives us only and everything good. So when I got sick with the measles after school one day, I remembered that I could get only good. And measles are not good. I put a sign over my bed: Measles Go Away. And my mom read stories to me about boys and girls who were saved from bad things. Before I went to sleep all the measles were gone.

KRISTIN GLATT

DAY FOUR

Silence gives you a minute to unwind before school. You can think about anything you want. Sometimes I say a short prayer. It's completely still.

PETER SIMA-EICHLER

DAY FIVE

Great God, with heart and tongue,
    To thee aloud we pray,
That all our children, while they're young,
    May walk in wisdom's way.

Now in their early days,
    Teach them thy will to know;
O God, thy sanctifying grace
    On every heart bestow.

Make their defenceless youth
   The object of thy care;
Cause them to choose the way of truth,
   And flee from every snare.

Their hearts to folly prone,
   Renew by power divine;
Unite them to thyself alone,
   And make them wholly thine.

Anonymous (19th Century)

Day Six

Today is another day to learn about God from the children around me. Today a child showed me a glimpse of God by:

Day Seven

Father-Mother Good,
Loving me
Guard me when I sleep
Guide my little feet up to thee.

Children's Evening Prayer, Mary Baker Eddy

Week
Nineteen

DAY ONE

Prayer, the language of spiritual sense, is the language we all innately speak. And it is understood, regardless of denomination or circumstance.

DAY TWO

As regards prayers for the sick, if any medical fact can be considered to stand firm, it is that in certain environments, prayer may contribute to recovery, and should be encouraged as a therapeutic measure.

WILLIAM JAMES, *The Varieties of Religious Experience*

DAY THREE

Sometimes an army of people is called together in prayer. I am one of those people who are occasionally asked to enlist in such an army. An organizer of our church's prayer chain called me one morning to enroll me in a prayer group that was coming together to pray for a young woman from a neighboring church. The girl had been in a car accident and her neck was broken. In that sort of accident it was a wonder she was alive long enough even for folks to organize to pray for her. Our church had decided to get involved in praying for others when one of our members pointed out that we had more faith in medicine than God. She had added that our church was more concerned with the drapes and the picnics than we were about our neighbors' well-being. What she said hit home with some of us, so we had called our neighbor churches from all denominations. We called the Presbyterian, Assembly of God, Methodist, Episcopal, and Pentecostal churches in our town and offered to join any prayer platoons they might have. It was this girl's car accident that brought us together in prayer with neighboring church groups. We all prayed, and it is no surprise that the girl recovered fully. Our church is now a different place. The drapes are not so important; God and prayer have returned to the center of our faith.

DAY FOUR

If anyone is healed by matter, through trusting in it, much more will he be healed by having recourse to the power of God. Why is he who trusts in the system of matter not willing to trust in God?

TATIAN

DAY FIVE

He said not: Thou shalt not be tempted, thou shalt not be travailed, thou shalt not be afflicted: but He said: Thou shalt not be overcome. God willeth that we take heed of these words, and that we be ever strong in such trust, in weal and woe. For He loveth and enjoyeth us, and so willeth He that we love and enjoy Him and mightily trust in Him, and all shall be well.

DAME JULIAN OF NORWICH

DAY SIX

The names of the people I can call on when I need prayer are:

DAY SEVEN

Affliction is a marvel of divine technique. It is a simple and ingenious device which introduces into the soul of a finite creature the immensity of force, blind, brutal, and cold. The infinite distance separating God from the creature is entirely concentrated into one point to pierce the soul in its center.

SIMONE WEIL

Week
Twenty

Day One

Spiritual sense is not confined to any geographic location and, like prayer, knows no boundaries, no walls, no borders, no time.

Day Two

Prayer is a medium of understanding the inner meaning of current events.

Dr. R. F. Horton

Day Three

Some time ago I woke up in a cold sweat and with the sudden knowledge that a certain country, Y, was about to be invaded by another country, X. There had been no hints of this in the news, no reason at all to normal sense that I should think this. But now I was in a panic. I bought a paper first thing in the morning to see if there was some news that would make sense of my night attack. There was a small item on a back page that said that country X was conducting summer military training maneuvers near the border of country Y. It looked like the prelude to an invasion. I called some friends and asked them what they thought. They hadn't heard of the situation and were not in the least interested nor alarmed. I couldn't sleep again that night. So I got out my Bible and started reading just for some peace and calm. And I came across the story of Elijah and Elisha, pursued by armies across the plains. Elisha is in a panic, and Elijah says to him, Don't be afraid, "Look up, for they that be with us are more than they that be with them." Elisha looked up, and the mountains were ringed with horses and chariots of fire.

One of those "click" moments overtook me. The horses and chariots of fire that Elijah pointed out translated in my mind to missiles that I knew surrounded the border of country Y. I was no longer afraid. I went to sleep with a feeling of safety. The newspaper two days later reported that the government of Y had called in some other governments with nuclear missles pointed toward country X. The "military maneuvers" were called off. I felt like a citizen of the world, a peacemaker, though I still don't know why the whole thing came to my mind at all.

DAY FOUR

Raise in yourself the Mind of Compassion
Help living beings
Abandon the will to fight
Wherever there is furious battle
Use all our might
To keep both sides' strength equal
And then step into the conflict to reconcile

Buddhist Sutra

DAY FIVE

Divine guidance must become the normal experience of ordinary men and women. Any man can pick up divine messages if he will put his receiving set in order. Definite, accurate, adequate information can come from the Mind of God to the minds of men. This is normal prayer. . . .

We accept as a commonplace a man's voice carried by radio to the uttermost parts of the earth. Why not the voice of the living God as an active, creative force in every home, every business, every parliament?

Frank Buchman

～

DAY SIX

Speak, Lord, for thy servant heareth. Grant us ears to hear, eyes to see, wills to obey, hearts to love; then declare what thou wilt, reveal what thou wilt, command what thou wilt, demand what thou wilt — Amen.

CHRISTINA G. ROSSETTI

～

DAY SEVEN

There is no change in the words of God.

No falsehood can enter it, in the past or future: a Revelation from a Most Wise, Praiseworthy.

KORAN 41:42

Absolute, we have revealed the reminder, and absolutely, we will preserve it.

KORAN 15:9

Week
Twenty-one

Day One

I spend too much time worrying. I complain about some government or other, I fuss about my neighbor's failings, I put up with a lurking dissatisfaction with my life. Instead of bemoaning the impotence of God and the flawed nature of His Creation I can credit the spiritual side of the ledger and Spirit's Ever-Present Love, which always acts to profit us all. I can refuse to believe in a whimsical male God who is out of touch with His Creation as easily as I can accept, instead, Spirit, eternally with us all.

Day Two

God, give us the grace to accept with serenity the things that cannot be changed, courage to change the things that should be changed, and wisdom to distinguish the one from the other.

REINHOLD NIEBUHR

DAY THREE

Let nothing disturb thee,
Nothing affright thee
All things are passing —
God never changeth.
Patient endurance
Attaineth to all things.
Who God possesseth
In nothing is wanting,
Alone God sufficeth.

ST. TERESA OF AVILA

DAY FOUR

There are two things in my life today that are unnecessary. They are:

I am eliminating them from my life this day.

DAY FIVE

Take therefore no thought for the morrow: for the morrow shall take thought for the things of itself. Sufficient unto the day is the evil thereof.

JESUS. MATTHEW 6:34

DAY SIX

God, thank you for giving me this very full moment. In this rich moment there is no sorrow, no pain. There is only the Love you are. Thank you for this moment.

DAY SEVEN

Neither shall they say, Lo here! or, lo there! for, behold, the kingdom of God is within you.

JESUS. LUKE 17:21

Week
Twenty-two

DAY ONE

We have no reason to be timid in our prayers and no reason to confine them merely to a theological setting. Prayer can usher us into places we have never been before, still the waves, annul any curse.

DAY TWO

They shall take up serpents; and if they drink any deadly thing, it shall not hurt them; they shall lay hands on the sick, and they shall recover.

JESUS. MARK 16:18

DAY THREE

Sometimes I almost "pray without ceasing," as they say, because I can't make it by myself, without God's help. I am in constant remembrance, and I'm forced to be in constant remembrance because I'm in so much need all the time. You have family, you have community life, you have business life; there's so many things going on. You're either in prayer of thanksgiving or in prayer of asking. Sometimes you just want to say, "Thank you, I know I'm fortunate." There are so many times when I'm thanking, but still I need this and I need that. I really know that God can perform and fulfill any need that I have.

CAROLE MU'MIN (in *How I Pray*, edited by Jim Castelli)

DAY FOUR

Do I think that God cannot deal with accidents?

What can I learn today about God that makes accidents yield to prayer?

DAY FIVE

On one spot I sit today
Others came, in ages past, to sit
One thousand years, still others will come.
Who is the singer, and who the listener?

NGUYEN CONG TRU

DAY SIX

There is no more natural event than prayer — knowing Love's allness.

DAY SEVEN

His name is an ointment poured forth.

SONG OF SOLOMON 1:3

Week
Twenty-three

DAY ONE

There are few places where we feel closer to God than in nature. Nature-worship and worship in nature are facts of our life on earth. Lakes are smiles of Spirit, trees the arms of God, the hints of life renewing itself season after season. The stars, the moon, the sun are symbols of the handiwork of Creation. Nature, in its glory, encourages us to pray and be at one with its elements.

DAY TWO

Truly precious are those things forming ladders reaching toward the beauty of the world, opening onto it.

The psalmist says:

He brought me forth also into a large place; he delivered me, because he delighted in me.

PSALM 18:19

DAY THREE

Spring Spiritualized

At length the opening spring has come,
　　How joyous is the scene!
The air is fill'd with rich perfume;
　　The fields are dressed in green.

I see my Saviour, from on high,
　　Break through the clouds and shine;
No creature now more blest than I,
　　No heart more glad than mine.

Thy word bids all my hopes revive,
　　It overcomes my foes;
It makes my drooping graces thrive,
　　And blossom like the rose.

Thus, Lord, a monument I stand
　　Of what thy grace can do;
Still guide me with thy gentle hand,
　　Thy changing seasons through.

The Mother's Hymnal Book

DAY FOUR

Summer's Queen, I am, the
Ultimate sustainer of life
Spectacular and lush, I

Treat my children with the fullness of my blessings
Adorning the whole of the land
In flower, leaf and fruit.
Now is the time of the early harvest —
I drown you in tomatoes and zucchini
Neighbors trade the superabundance
Grown in the warmth of my smile.

Magnificent Mother am I, and I call you to
Observe My Season. Open your Self to
the rays of my summer sun — lie on beaches,
Enjoy the fruits of my blessings
Radiating down upon the earth.

FERN BERNSTEIN-MILLER

DAY FIVE

Streaks of sunlight pour over a darkening Sea
Slightly outlining clouds in silver
While the sun sinks in silent mystery
Beyond the horizon.

It's the time of quiet breezes,
Of waves that whisper their souls on beaches
    made of gold.

The solititude, the gentle peace
Wash over me. Facing the setting sun
Taking a deep breath, I lose myself.

I blend into the surrounding quiet,
Whisper in the waves and swirl

Joyously in the breezes; becoming
Part of the natural innocence and Simplicity that
   is.

By losing myself in the greater reality,
I understand that life is only how it is
Perceived.

The only name reality has is the one we give it.

CAROLYN MALONEY

⁓

DAY SIX

Consider a flower. Hold one in your hand. Ponder it. Compose a prayer on the beauty of the flower. Soul and its attributes are beyond description, but not beyond recognition.

⁓

DAY SEVEN

They shall fear thee as long as the sun and moon endure throughout all generations. He shall come down like rain upon the mown grass: as showers that water the earth. In his days shall the righteous flourish; and abundance of peace so long as the moon endureth.

PSALM 72:5–7

Week
Twenty-four

DAY ONE

Anxiety about the future is a symptom of the times. Will we keep our jobs, our husbands, our lovers? Will we have children, and if we have children will they grow safely into fully responsible adults? What of our parents? Our health? Where will we grow old? Will we?

We can assure ourselves by catching a glimpse of the Allness of God, expressed by the psalmist:

Where can I go from your Spirit? Where can I flee from your presence? If I go up to the heavens, you are there; if I make my bed in the depths, you are there. If I rise on the wings of the dawn, if I settle on the far side of the sea, even there your hand will guide me, your right hand will hold me fast.

PSALM 139:7–10
New International Version

DAY TWO

Do not be impatient in times of dryness and darkness; allow the removals and delays of the consolations of God; draw near to Him and wait upon Him patiently that your life may be increased and renewed.

APOCRYPHA, *A New Day: Daily Readings for Our Times.*

DAY THREE

The experiences of other people can speak to us deeply even though their circumstances are radically different. I read of a young woman who was a prisoner of war in a German prison camp in the first years of World War II.

She told how she sat on the floor under the one light in a room of prisoners and read the Bible and *Science and Health* [Mary Baker Eddy] day and night. She wrote that at one point it was just as if a door had been left open and she saw that man — as he really is — cannot be detained in a prison, because he is as unlimited and unbounded as God.

As I read her story I glimpsed her freedom. The woman said that after her moment of revelation she picked up the books and a few personal things and walked out of the prison camp in broad daylight. She walked past the guards and the towers and the tanks and no one saw her or came after her.

I think about this woman from another generation and another time and marvel at the freedom she saw for a brief moment and experienced for the rest of her life.

DAY FOUR

Thou shalt not be afraid for the terror by night; nor for the arrow that flieth by day; nor for the pestilence that walketh in darkness; nor for the destruction that wasteth at noonday.

PSALM 91:5–6

DAY FIVE

The deep unrest, uneasiness and alarm at the effects of our modern civilization, the increasing hollowness and precariousness of conventional values, the derangement of human relations, all strike at our deepest being. The loss of religion and, with it, the firm personal foundation of values, of an understandable cosmic order and hierarchy of beings; the loss of a person's established outer and inner status; the loss of orientation in the maze of the modern world, the loss of meaning, of inner security, the feelings of forsakenness, anxiety and alienation — prayers that address these conditions as well as the eternal questions of life and death are in great demand. It's never too soon for prayers to meet the anxiety we all face when we think about tomorrow.

~

DAY SIX

Lord, why should I doubt any more, when you have given me such assured pledges of your love? First, you are my Creator, I your creature, you my master, I your servant. But hence arises not my comfort: you my Father, I your child. "You shall be my sons and daughters," says the Lord Almighty. Christ is my brother: "I ascend to my Father and your Father, to my God and your God; but, lest this should not be enough your maker is your husband." Nay, more, I am a member of his body, my head. Such privileges — had not the Word of truth made them know who or where is the man that dared in his heart to have presumed to have thought it? So wonderful are these thoughts that my spirit fails in me on their consideration, and I am confounded to think that God, who has done so much for me, should have so little from me. But this is no comfort, that when I come to heaven, I shall understand perfectly what he has done for me, and then I shall be able to praise him as

I ought. Lord, having this hope let me purify myself as you are pure, and let me be no more afraid of death, but even desire to be dissolved and be with you which is best of all.

ANNE BRADSTREET

DAY SEVEN

For I know the plans I have for you declares the Lord, plans to prosper you and not to harm you, plans to give you hope and a future.

JEREMIAH 29:11

Week
Twenty-five

DAY ONE

Sh'ma Yisrael — Hear O Israel — is the call of God speaking through the centuries. Reflecting on the prayer that accompanies the call enriches each day of this week.

Sh'ma, Yisrael
The Lord is One.

His dominion is without limit,
boundless in space, endless in time.

Adonai Ehad.

God's unity encompasses life and death,
heaven and earth, light and darkness.

The Lord is One.

The sum of all that has been,
the promise of all that is to be.

Adonai Ehad.

God's Oneness unites us with all nature,
the smallest grain of sand with the farthest star.

The Lord is One.

God's unity is sensed in the struggle
for human harmony, for harmony with nature.

Adonai Ehad.

We make God's purposes our own
when we dedicate body and soul to His service,
when we attain that love of other creatures
which is at one with the love of God.

SIDDUR SIM SHALOM

DAY TWO

I reflect that:

His dominion is without limit
boundless in space, endless in time.

DAY THREE

I reflect that:

God's unity encompasses life and death,
heaven and earth, light and darkness.

～

DAY FOUR

I reflect that:

The sum of all that has been,
the promise of all that is to be.

～

DAY FIVE

I reflect that:

God's Oneness unites us with all nature,
the smallest grain of sand with the farthest star.

～

DAY SIX

I reflect that:

God's unity is sensed in the struggles for human
harmony, for harmony with nature.

DAY SEVEN

I reflect that:

We make God's purposes our own
when we dedicate body and soul to His service,
when we attain that love of other creatures
which is at one with the love of God.

Week
Twenty-six

DAY ONE

Music is a language of prayer. From the "Ode to Joy" in the last movement of Beethoven's Ninth Symphony, to the Psalms, from the snippets of popular love songs that linger in our thought, to hymns, to the nursery rhymes of the innocent child, song is prayer. While one may not know by heart the poet Friedrich Schiller's words to the "Ode to Joy," or be able to sing Beethoven's music, one can always find a song to sing.

DAY TWO

We can't choose happiness either for ourselves or for another; we can't tell where that will lie. We can only choose whether we will indulge ourselves in the present moment, or whether we will renounce that, for the sake of obeying the Divine voice within us, — for the sake of being true to all the motives that sanctify our lives. I know this belief is hard; it has slipped away from me again and again; but I have felt that if I let it go forever, I should have no light through the darkness of this life.

GEORGE ELIOT

⁓

DAY THREE

When I first began prayer as a way of living, I really didn't have much of a clue about how it worked, or what my part in the dialogue ought to be. And I didn't know, or think to learn, how others had prayed before me. What I *did* do in those early days was memorize some hymns. I often felt trapped, unsure, victimized by another's moods and money. I wanted out, and so every day for a year I sang words written by Anna L. Waring, another woman in another time, until they came true for me — which they did.

In heavenly Love abiding,
No change my heart shall fear;
And safe is such confiding,
For nothing changes here.
The storm may roar without me,
My heart may low be laid;
But God is round about me,
And can I be dismayed?

Wherever He may guide me,
No want shall turn me back;
My shepherd is beside me,
And nothing can I lack,
His wisdom ever waketh,
His sight is never dim;
He knows the way He taketh,
And I will walk with Him.

Green pastures are before me,
Which yet I have not seen,
Bright skies will soon be o'er me,
Where darkest clouds have been.
My hope I cannot measure,
My path in life is free;
My Father has my treasure,
And He will walk with me.

DAY FOUR

If I had to choose one song to sing to God it would be:

DAY FIVE

Sing unto the Lord; for he hath done excellent things: this is known in all the earth.

ISAIAH 12:5

I will sing unto the Lord as long as I live: I will sing praise to my God while I have my being.

PSALM 104:33

DAY SIX

When Israel was in Egypt's Land,
Let my people go;
Oppressed so hard they could not stand,
Let my people go.

Chorus:
Go down, Moses, way down in Egypt's Land;
Tell old Pharaoh
Let my people go.

Thus saith the Lord, bold Moses said.
Let my people go.
If not I'll smite your firstborn dead,
Let my people go.

Chorus.

We need not always weep and mourn
Let my people go.
And wear these slavery chains forlorn.
Let my people go.

Chorus.

African-American Spiritual

DAY SEVEN

O daughter of Zion, awake from thy sadness;
Awake, for thy foes shall oppress thee no more.

Hymn (author unknown)

Week
Twenty-seven

DAY ONE

Praise is natural. We cannot restrain praise when things are going our way, when the day is wonderful beyond description. Praise is prayer.

DAY TWO

. . . And Jesus lifted up his eyes, and said, Father, I thank thee that thou hast heard me.

JOHN 11:41

DAY THREE

Julie Krone was the first jockey in 20 years and only the third in 126 years to win five races in one day at the Saratoga Race Course.

"When I pulled up after the ninth race, I really and truly looked up to heaven and said, 'Thank you, God.'

"You can't, in terms of putting it into words, explain how special it is to win five races here. It's so special that it just made me think that maybe God really did have something to do with it."

~

DAY FOUR

Silent longing is prayer.
A wish is a prayer.
Craving is prayer.
Desire is prayer.
Longing, hungering and yearning are the companions of prayer. Prayer is desire to get out of terrible situations, desire to praise, desire to know oneself, desire to know God.

~

DAY FIVE

Through the ages the wise agree we need prayers that bring us more grace, patience, common sense and a wholesome perception of God's requirements.

~

DAY SIX

Rabbinical wisdom says that every person can see God according to his or her own nature: one in weeping, one in prayer and one in songs of praise.

DAY SEVEN

What do you desire?
That is your prayer.

Week
Twenty-eight

DAY ONE

We take self-examination as a matter of course when it comes to our bodies. What about a daily self-examination of our spiritual sense? What are the ingredients of a spiritual self-examination? How much time would it take to examine, and where would we look?

DAY TWO

Looking in the mirror has never made me happy. There is always something I don't like or that seems wrong. To avoid that nagging preoccupation, I now shower, brush my hair and teeth, get dressed and say to myself, "Now you are taken care of, leave me alone for the rest of the day so I can get on with my life." This simple ritual has given me much more time for spiritual satisfaction.

DAY THREE

When a feeling or thought arises, your intention should not be to chase it away, even by continuing to concentrate on the breath; the feeling or thought passes naturally from the mind. The intention isn't to chase it away, hate it, worry about it, or be frightened by it. Simply acknowledge its presence. For example when a feeling of sadness arises, simply recognize it: "A feeling of sadness has just arisen in me." If the feeling of sadness continues, continue to recognize: "A feeling of sadness is still in me." The essential thing is not to let any feeling or thought arise without recognizing it in mindfulness, like a palace guard who is aware of every face that passes through the front door.

When I mentioned the guard — perhaps you imagined a front corridor with two doors, one entrance and one exit, with your mind as the guard. Whatever feeling or thought enters, you are aware of its entrance, and when it leaves you are aware of its exit. But the image has a shortcoming; it suggests that those who enter and exit the corridor are different from the guard. In fact our thoughts and feelings are us. They are a part of ourselves. There is a temptation to look upon them, or at least some of them, as an enemy force which is trying to disturb the concentration and understanding of your mind. But, in fact, when we are angry, we ourselves are anger. When we are happy, we ourselves are happiness. When we have certain thoughts we ourselves are those thoughts. We are both the guard and the visitor at the same time.

THICH NHAT HANH, *The Miracle of Mindfulness*

〜

DAY FOUR

There is no reason to neglect our individual spiritual selves. Examining ourselves, we may ask; why do we pray? Is our motivation to tell God something God might not already know? If we pray to be noticed and appreciated for our devotion we may not get what we ask for. And if God already knows everything, then it's not necessary to remind the All Divine. But when we pray what God already knows then we are in accord with God and we experience the harmony, truth and love of God.

If we think of God as only a big person, whether male or female, we are defining God by limited physical senses. But God is known only through spiritual sense. God's standard is that God is the same yesterday, today and forever. And that is not just a lovely statement but a profound fact.

〜

DAY FIVE

Have mercy upon me, O God, according to thy loving kindness: according unto the multitude of thy tender mercies blot out my transgressions. Wash me throughly from mine iniquity, and cleanse me from my sin. . . . Behold, thou desirest truth in the inward parts: and in the hidden part thou shalt make me to know wisdom. Purge me with hyssop, and I shall be clean: wash me, and I shall be whiter than snow. . . . Create in me a clean heart, O God; and renew a right spirit within me.

PSALM 51:1–2, 6–7, 10

DAY SIX

Self-righteousnesss, gloom, pessimism, anxiety, unbalanced or unreasonable criticism of the culture, all are evidence of a deficient defense against attacks on spiritual identity. Never forget, as you pray, that Spirit endows you. As far as Spirit is concerned all there is to you is the activity of Spirit. This activity is eternally maintained. It doesn't ebb and flow depending on the Almighty's mood — or yours for that matter.

DAY SEVEN

The king's daughter is all glorious within. . . .

PSALM 45:13

Week
Twenty-nine

DAY ONE

How far have I come on the path of prayer? I can use this list to remind myself that:

- Prayer works.
- Prayer is practical religion.
- Prayer takes sincerity.
- Prayer is not merely the murmuring of pleasant phrases, nor the grand shout of help; although both those things are prayer.
- Prayer is a turning of the self inside out.
- Prayer is the full person's height of aspiration.
- Prayer shows us that God's law is supreme over man's law.
- Prayer that resonates in the heart and speaks humbly, shines through the ages.
- Prayer activates in our lives the Divine Truth that annihilates evil, sickness and fear.

DAY TWO

There is an etiquette to prayer. We pray for ourselves and for those in authority. We pray for those who ask; and we pray for children not old enough to ask. We pray for those who are unconscious. We do *not* pray for those *we* think need prayer unless they ask us to.

DAY THREE

How to Pray

1. Be humble
2. Be honest
3. Give up bitterness and resentment
4. Say no to fear
5. Say *yes* to the constants of prayer: God is All
6. Thank God
7. Be at rest

DAY FOUR

We already know how to speak the language of prayer. We simply need to practice it.

I will practice today.

DAY FIVE

The results of my prayer practice of yesterday:

DAY SIX

A hint of the presence of active prayer is the clear feeling of safety.

DAY SEVEN

Almighty God, bestow upon us the meaning of words, the light of understanding, the nobility of diction and the faith of the true nature. And grant that what we believe we may also speak.

SAINT HILARY

Week
Thirty

DAY ONE

I believe in God the Father Almighty, Maker of heaven and earth:

And in Jesus Christ his only Son our Lord: Who was conceived by the Holy Ghost, Born of the Virgin Mary: Suffered under Pontius Pilate, Was crucified, dead, and buried: He descended into hell; The third day he rose again from the dead: He ascended into heaven, And sitteth on the right hand of God the Father Almighty: From thence he shall come to judge the quick and the dead.

I believe in the Holy Ghost: the holy Catholic Church; The Communion of Saints; The Forgiveness of sins: The Resurrection of the body: And the Life everlasting. Amen.

The Apostles' Creed
The Book of Common Prayer (1979)

DAY TWO

Almighty God, who hast given us grace at this time with one accord to make our common supplications unto thee; and dost promise that when two or three are gathered together in thy Name thou wilt grant their requests; Fulfil now, O Lord, the desires and petitions of thy servants, as may be most expedient for them; granting us in this world knowledge of thy truth, and in the world to come life everlasting. Amen.

A Prayer of Saint Chrysostom
The Book of Common Prayer (1928)

DAY THREE

Lord, have mercy upon us
Christ, have mercy upon us.
Lord, have mercy upon us.

The Book of Common Prayer

DAY FOUR

O God of Abraham, God of Isaac, God of Jacob, bless these thy servants, and sow the seed of eternal life in their minds, that whatsoever in thy holy word they shall profitably learn, they may in deed fulfill the same.

The Book of Common Prayer (1559)
(from The Solemnization of Matrimony)

DAY FIVE

Be not wise in your own conceits. Recompense to no man evil for evil. Provide things honest in the sight of all men. Dearly beloved, avenge not yourselves, but rather give place unto wrath: for it is written, Vengeance is mine; I will repay, saith the Lord. Therefore if thine enemy hunger, feed him; if he thirst, give him drink: for in so doing thou shalt heap coals of fire upon his head. Be not overcome of evil, but overcome evil with good.

The Book of Common Prayer (1928)
(reading from Romans 12:16–12 for the third Sunday after Epiphany)

DAY SIX

O Lord, we beseech thee mercifully to receive the prayers of thy people who call upon thee; and grant that they may both perceive and know what things they ought to do, and also may have grace and power faithfully to fulfil the same; through Jesus Christ our Lord. Amen.

The Book of Common Prayer (1928)
(Collect for the first Sunday after Epiphany)

DAY SEVEN

Lord, we pray thee that thy grace may always precede and follow us, and make us continually to be given to all good works; through Jesus Christ our Lord, who liveth and reigneth with thee and the Holy Spirit, one God, now and for ever. Amen.

The Book of Common Prayer (1979)
(Collect for the seventeenth Sunday after Trinity)

Week Thirty-one

DAY ONE

God does not require enormous faith but an accurate faith.

~

DAY TWO

Study to shew thyself approved unto God, a workman that needeth not to be ashamed, rightly dividing the word of truth.

2 TIMOTHY 2:15

~

DAY THREE

Martha had a child in the morning preschool that I ran for a few children in town. I had mentioned to her how a stranger's prayer had healed my son of asthma. She did not seem impressed one way or another, but one day she called and said, "Do you think prayer would work to bring rain? We haven't had

rain in this valley for over six months and cattle are
dying, there is no water for my horses, my crops are
withering, all that biblical stuff, and I wondered?
Shouldn't you be praying for rain?"

Not having cattle or sheep or crops other than my
own garden I hadn't thought much about rain. And
it was so early in my prayer life that I hadn't done
much but look through the Bible Psalms, read some
in a few other books and begin to memorize some
hymns. I certainly did not know how to pray for rain.
But I did think I would find out what rain was —
biblically speaking. I began reading each Bible verse
where the word "rain" appeared — beginning with
the first — Genesis 2:5 and then to Genesis 7:4; the
account of Noah and the forty days and nights that
"rain was upon the earth." I read on to Deuteronomy, to Job ("hath the rain a father?") and
through the major and minor prophets until I came
to the reference in Matthew: "he sendeth rain on the
just and the unjust." It looked to me that rain is
impartial. By 5:30 P.M. the sky was dark and the
wind was blowing and at around 6:00 it started to
pour.

It was still pouring next morning when Martha
called and said she couldn't bring her child in to
nursery school because the roads were flooded out
where she was. And she called the following day to
say, "Now how about praying for it to stop?"

What I was most grateful for was to learn that the

Bible is not a compilation of literal aphorisms but a textbook that educates thought out of literalness into some really interesting concepts that have practical application.

⁓

Day Four

We know that God knows our needs before we ask. Being specific about what we are praying for helps us to know what we are asking for, so, in prayer, we address the specific need.

⁓

Day Five

Abba, Abba-Father
Help me to plant
A garden for You

Mystical flowers
Seeded by virtues
Nourished by loving
Strengthened by trials

Your Light and your water
Giving it life
Blooming inside me
For You to enjoy

Abba, Abba-Father
Within this garden
May together we live
I as your child
You as my God

DESIREE BRASSETTE

DAY SIX

We do not stand in front of a blackboard and pray to understand mathematics. We learn the principles of arithmetic, we study the multiplication tables, and *then* we solve the problem. Why do we think prayer is different?

DAY SEVEN

Hast thou entered into the treasures of the snow? or hast thou seen the treasures of the hail, which I have reserved against the time of trouble . . . ?

JOB 38:22–23

Week
Thirty-two

DAY ONE

Prayer acknowledges realities belonging to the Divine Mind. Accompanying this admission is the refusal — which is part of admitting how things really are — to accept anything unlike God, good, love for ourselves and for everyone.

DAY TWO

There is a school of thought that says when we are physically ill, what we suffer from is discord in our lives and not the illness. If this is so, then we should admit only spiritual facts and our eternal connection to God. Prayer is the spiritual acknowledging of the ever-present intelligence and love of God — a spiritual metaphysics that tells us which school of thought is true and which is not.

~⸜

DAY THREE

I had been living in Asia for some years. The garden was warm and the air sticky as I watered the orchids hanging from the trees. The thought came to me, "I am a butterfly." All the boundaries of my human self seemed to be gone. It took effort to pull myself out of whatever it was that had overtaken me. "The Lord is my Shepherd" is all I could think of to help pull me back into my body and the house. My identity is individual and eternal and not subject to culture, environment or location.

~⸜

DAY FOUR

The development of the personal self, and treating it as a number one priority in a world of other mortals is a world apart from the development of a prayerful self. In genuine prayer the Self is silent. It is God who speaks.

~⸜

DAY FIVE

Who do I think I am?

Day Six

And, behold, one came and said unto him, Good Master, what good thing shall I do, that I may have eternal life? And he said unto him, Why callest thou me good? there is none good but one, that is, God: but if thou wilt enter into life, keep the commandments.

MATTHEW 19:16–17

Day Seven

I the Lord am your God who brought you out of the land of Egypt, the house of bondage: You shall have no gods besides Me.

EXODUS 20:2
Tanakh — The Holy Scriptures

Week
Thirty-three

Day One

Conventional wisdom says the way to get a message across is to repeat it and repeat it, but evil repeated is not evil validated. The perpetual expression of evil would present itself again and again. The antidote to evil's iteration, says Scripture, is, "O earth, earth, earth hear the word of the Lord." (Jeremiah 22:29)

~

Day Two

It has been said that there is of nothing so much in hell as of self-will. For hell is nothing but self-will, and if there were no self-will there would be no devil and no hell. When it is said that Lucifer fell from Heaven, and turned away from God, and the like, it means nothing else than that he would have his own will, and would not be of one will with the Eternal Will. So it was likewise with Adam in Paradise. And when we say self-will we mean: To will otherwise than as the One and Eternal Will of God wills.

Theologia Germanica

DAY THREE

I never understood evil. And I still don't. I couldn't understand why my husband was beating me. And I couldn't understand why it seemed there was no place to escape him. And one day it just occurred to me that evil simply could not be understood. There was no explanation at all for it. It seemed very clear to me and the next day my husband told me to get out and I did. And that was the end of the beating, the marriage and that particular evil in my life.

DAY FOUR

The Lord spoke to Moses, saying, "Send men to scout the land of Canaan, which I am giving to the Israelite people." (Numbers 13:1–2)

When Moses sent them to scout the land of Canaan he said to them, "Go up there into the Negeb and on into the hill country, and see what kind of country it is. Are the people who dwell in it strong or weak, few or many?" (13: 17–18)

At the end of forty days they returned from scouting the land. (13:25)

This is what they told him: "We came to the land you sent us to; it does indeed flow with milk and honey, and this is its fruit. However, the people who inhabit the country are powerful, and the cities are fortified and very large. . . ." (13:27–28)

Caleb hushed the people before Moses and said, "Let us by all means go up, and we shall gain possession of it, for we shall surely overcome it." But the men who had gone up with him said, "We cannot attack that people, for it is stronger than we. . . . The country that we traversed and scouted is one that devours its settlers. All the people that we saw in it are men of great size; . . . and we looked like grasshoppers to ourselves, and so we must have looked to them." (13:30–33)

BOOK OF NUMBERS
Tanakh — The Holy Scriptures

DAY FIVE

We reinterpret sense impressions so constantly that we don't even know we are doing it. Distant objects are not as small as our eye tells us they are. Proportion and size are reinterpretations of physical sight. Spiritual sight tells us how to size up situations as they really are.

DAY SIX

"The Lord will battle for you; you hold your peace!"

EXODUS 14:14
Tanakh: The Holy Scriptures

DAY SEVEN

We call the evil good, and the good evil (Isaiah 5:20), we can never be honest with ourselves completely, can we?

MADAME GUYON

Week
Thirty-four

Day One

In one sense, when we are healed, what we are healed of is not a headache or a broken marriage or a depleted bank account but misconceptions of who we are and the state of our spiritual health or relationships.

Day Two

Heal us, Lord, and we shall be healed, save us, and we shall be saved; for it is You we praise. Send relief and healing for all our diseases, our sufferings and our wounds, for You are a merciful and faithful healer. Blessed are You, Lord, who heals the sick.

SIDDUR SIM SHALOM

DAY THREE

I was working in a public maternity hospital. On many occasions I was faced with dire situations. All the medical help available had been given, and yet the child was going downhill. It seemed so wrong, so unjust! Something in me rebelled. Then I'd ask myself, What is truly going on here? As I looked away from the human picture of a small, frail physical infant to see the child of God — strong and whole, already perfect — the child would recover. I was learning to acknowledge God's very tangible presence and goodness and seeing the effect of such spiritualized thought.

JER MASTER, CSB

DAY FOUR

The power of the physician's belief system to shape the patient's responses to therapy is akin to prayer. Both prayer and belief are nonlocal manifestations of consciousness, because both can operate at a distance, sometimes outside the patient's awareness. Both affirm that "it's not all physical" and both can be used adjunctively with other forms of therapy.

LARRY DOSSEY, M.D. *Healing Words: The Power of Prayer and the Practice of Medicine*

~

DAY FIVE

Ask your doctor about cases of healing through prayer with the same confidence you would ask her where she took her internship or where she studied.

~

DAY SIX

In prayer or receipt of good, some ailment fades out or disappears, talents surface we didn't know we had, we relate better to others. We have more of the things we need and perhaps we are more appreciative of what we have. Our interests and hobbies put down deeper roots. Our analysis of business problems becomes more acute, we develop more workable solutions and we don't need to run away. We don't need to break down and collapse with self-pity.

~

DAY SEVEN

Remember not, Lord, our iniquities, nor the iniquities of our forefathers: Spare us, good Lord, spare thy people, whom thou hast redeemed with thy most precious blood, and be not angry with us for ever.

Spare us, good, Lord.

The Book of Common Prayer (1892)
(from The Visitation of the Sick)

DAY ONE

Lord thou knowest better than I know myself that I am growing older and will someday be old.

Keep me from getting talkative and particularly from the fatal habit of thinking I must say something on every occasion.

Release me from craving to try to straighten out everybody's affairs.

Keep my mind free from the recital of endless details — give me wings to get to the point.

I ask for grace enough to listen to the tales of others' pains. Help me to endure them with patience but seal my lips on my own aches and pains — they are increasing, and my love of rehearsing them is becoming sweeter as the years go by.

Teach me the lovely lesson that occasionally it is possible that I may be mistaken.

Keep me reasonably sweet. I do not want to be a saint — some of them are so hard to live with — but a sour old person is one of the crowning works of the devil. Make me thoughtful but not moody; helpful, but not bossy. With my vast store of wisdom it seems

a pity not to use it all — but thou knowest Lord that
I want a few friends at the end.

Author Unknown

DAY TWO

Prayer for Grandparents

Most loving God,
we ask your blessing
upon our grandparents.
They connect us
with the generations before us
and remind us of our responsibility
to the generations to come
for whom we shall be their ancestors.
Bless our grandparents
with loving families,
with good health,
with compassionate and tender friends.
Grant us the wisdom to give unto them
honor, respect and love
that their days may be a blessing.
In the name of Christ we pray.
Amen.

VIENNA COBB ANDERSON

DAY THREE

What do I want at the end of my life?

DAY FOUR

And, behold, there was a man in Jerusalem, whose name was Simeon; and the same man was just and devout, waiting for the consolation of Israel: and the Holy Ghost was upon him.

LUKE 2:25–26

DAY FIVE

And there was one Anna, a prophetess, the daughter of Phanuel, of the tribe of Asher: she was of great age, and had lived with her husband seven years from her virginity; and she was a widow of about fourscore and four years, which departed not from the temple, but served God with fastings and prayers night and day. And she coming in that insant gave thanks likewise unto the Lord, and spake of him to all them that looked for redemption in Jerusalem.

LUKE 2:26–38

DAY SIX

God's, the Kingdom of the Heavens and of the Earth: and unto God the final return!

KORAN 105:24

DAY SEVEN

Thank you for the joy of living.
Thank you for the blessing of love.
Thank you for the comfort of friendship
Thank you for the kindness of strangers.
Thank you for the freedom to make choices.
Thank you for the wonderment of opportunity.
Thank you for the excitement of challenges.
Thank you for the wisdom learned in failures.
Thank you for new beginnings.
Thank you for fulfilled endings.

Author Unknown

Week
Thirty-six

DAY ONE

Because Sir Isaac Newton, who formulated the law of gravity, was English doesn't mean that gravity is English. It's the same with prayer. The spiritual laws upon which prayer is based do not depend on nationality, race, religion or gender.

DAY TWO

Love worketh no ill to his neighbor: therefore love is the fulfilling of the law.

ROMANS 13:10

DAY THREE

When I was very young I thought I had to obey every whim of every person on earth. As I grew older I realized that the only law was Divine. Allowing myself to be dominated was breaking God's law, and causing other people to break God's law. With age and maturity I study Divine law as if I were perpetually in law school — which is as it truly is.

DAY FOUR

Prayer is the expression in human language of Divine knowledge.

DAY FIVE

Prayer requires obedience to Divine law, but where we have little problem obeying traffic laws, or paying our income tax, we do not have such an easy time obeying God's law. Do we love our neighbor? Do we expect good? Do our prayers sustain us in understanding Divine law?

Shouldn't they?

DAY SIX

One law of God that I can meditate upon and obey today is:

Day Seven

But the fruit of the Spirit is love, joy, peace, long suffering, gentleness, goodness, faith, meekness, temperance: against such there is no law.

Galatians 5:22–23

Week
Thirty-seven

DAY ONE

Prayers are like recipes: they come packaged or are made from scratch; they have "ingredients" — certain amounts of this, particular amounts of that, mixed, stirred, blended, tossed. Sometimes, like recipes, prayers are meant for public approval — for the oohs and aahs we hope to receive when we offer up our "creation." Sometimes recipes, like prayers, are created in a moment of deep desire or hunger for a particular taste. Even if you are not what you might call a "good" cook — the recipe and the right ingredients produce at least a passing resemblance to what you had in mind. So too with prayer.

DAY TWO

In many faiths, one washes one's hands before prayer. In prayer, as in cooking, you don't bring the dirt from your previous work to the process. I wanted to remind myself that prayer is a sweet scent offered to God that washes clean the accumulation of the senses. This recipe is from a family cookbook.

Attar of Roses

> Three handfuls dried rose petals
> Almond oil

In a heat-proof glass jar, put the rose petals and barely cover with the oil. Put the jar in a pan of simmering water until the oil has removed all the color of the petals. Strain, and discard petals.

Keep liquid in the tightly sealed jar. May be kept chilled in the refrigerator if desired. Use to wash hands or dab with cotton on face as freshner.

DAY THREE

I pray while I cook. Not to make a better meal, but because it brings me peace. It is a time to really think about each ingredient of the meal, a time to see how wonderful something made with simple elements can become. It's a time to get out of myself.

One of my favorite meals is the simplest to prepare. I pour some olive oil in a skillet so that the oil is about an eighth of an inch deep and I think of the uses of oil. Oil was used to anoint Jesus, oil is a sign of consecration and, in another form, oil forms much of the basis of many economies. I slice three or four garlic cloves and think of Creation and how each plant or fruit or vegetable has a flavor and distinctness, and I remind myself that I am part of that Creation. I boil water and think of the Spirit of God moving on the face of the waters, and while some linguini is cooking in the boiling water I cut a few Roma tomatoes into quarters and scrape them and the garlic off the cutting board into the heated oil. Just after the tomatoes and garlic have gone into the olive oil, I drain the pasta and then scoop it in with the oil, tomatoes and garlic. I stir it once, take it right out of the pan and put it onto a plate. After adding some grated Romano cheese and a few basil leaves on top I am ready to sit down and say grace.

Once the water has boiled the whole procedure doesn't take more than ten minutes in my kitchen but in my prayers and meditations I have traveled to lands where olive trees grow, to the time of Jesus, to the Middle East today, to the eternality of Creation where the "seed is within itself."

~

DAY FOUR

Whenever you get a recipe from someone ask them for their favorite prayer or meditation too. Write the recipe on one side of your cookbook page, or card, and the prayer or meditation on the other.

When you send out a recipe from your kitchen, send a prayer or meditation with it.

~

DAY FIVE

Then said the Lord unto Moses, Behold, I will rain bread from heaven for you. . . .

EXODUS 16:4

And the house of Israel called the name thereof Manna; and it was like coriander seed, white; and the taste of it was like wafers made with honey.

EXODUS 16:31

~

DAY SIX

When Jesus then lifted up his eyes, and saw a great company come unto him, he saith unto Philip, Whence shall we buy bread that these may eat? And this he said to prove him: for he himself knew what he would do.

One of his disciples, Andrew, Simon Peter's brother, saith unto him, There is a lad here, which hath five barley loaves and two small fishes; but what are they among so many?

And Jesus took the loaves; and when he had given

thanks, he distributed to the disciples, and the disciples to them that were set down; and likewise of the fishes as much as they would. When they were filled, he said unto his disciples, Gather up the fragments that remain, that nothing be lost. . . . Therefore they gathered them together, and filled twelve baskets with the fragments of the five barley loaves, which remained over and above unto them that had eaten.

JOHN 6:5–6, 8–9, 11–13

DAY SEVEN

O taste and see that the Lord is good. . . .

PSALM 34:8.

Week
❦ Thirty-eight ❧

Day One

One way to pray is to write a thank-you letter to God. Get out your best stationery and your best pen. Clean off your desk or table, or sit under a tree in the midst of nature. Today is the day to write God a letter of prayer.

Day Two

My heart is inditing a good matter: I speak of the things which I have made touching the king: my tongue is the pen of a ready writer.

PSALM 45:1

Day Three

A thank-you note to God might include gratitude for what you already have. Get your heart, not only your tongue, into it.

There are a thousand things to be grateful for. Begin listing them here.

⁓

DAY FOUR

How creative can I be in my thank-you note to the Creator? Perfunctory thank-you notes are obligatory and the receiver knows it. Creative ways to say thank you for a specific gift are always treasured.

⁓

DAY FIVE

Children who write thank-you notes are the first to receive more presents.

Write every thank-you note as if it were a note to one of God's daughters or sons, who might at any moment read the note to her Father or Mother.

⁓

DAY SIX

Paul's salutation in his first letter to the church at Corinth:

Paul, called to be an apostle of Jesus Christ through the will of God, and Sosthenes our brother, unto the church which is at Corinth, to them that are sanctified in Christ Jesus, called to be saints, with all that in every place call upon the name of Jesus Christ our Lord, both theirs and ours: Grace be unto you, and peace from God our Father, and from the Lord Jesus Christ.

1 CORINTHIANS 1:1–3

DAY SEVEN

I have written my letter to God with the certainty that it will be received and heard.

Week
Thirty-nine

Day One

Prayers for safety, prayers for courage are found in every tradition, for it is when we don't know what else to do that we most often turn to prayer. The language of prayer for safekeeping varies over time and, to some degree, with gender. Each of us must learn our own prayers for safekeeping in our own tongue and in our own time.

Day Two

He that dwelleth in the secret place of the most High shall abide under the shadow of the Almighty. I will say of the Lord, He is my refuge and my fortress: my God; in him will I trust.

Psalm 91:1–2

⌒

DAY THREE

I'd spent the morning in prayer. In the afternoon I had gone to a carnival in a city park, with the children and my fiancée. Everything seemed fine for a while. I was looking at the man running the Ferris wheel and watching him as he bent over, a cigarette dangling from his mouth, when all of a sudden the scene shifted. I could see him hit a man and a fight break out. But I knew he hadn't hit a man, because when I looked again, everything was the same as it had been the second before the scene changed. "We have to leave," I said to my fiancée. There is going to be a fight here and it is going to become very dangerous. And though there was absolutely no evidence (other than that one fleeting glimpse I had), my fiancée said, "Fine."

We explained to the children we had changed our minds about the rest of the carnival and that we were going to the beach instead. We drove to the beach, and as we got ready to park and turn off the radio there was an emergency announcement: A fight had broken out at the Ferris wheel of the carnival and six people had been killed, a fire had been set and that part of the city was aflame.

DAY FOUR

Saved
Rescued from a red hot suffocating
rage
By the fluttering presence of a solitary angel

Who encircled me with white
embracing light
That becalmed me like a soft
billowing breeze
And made me spiritually safe

Thank you universe.

FREDERICA DALY

DAY FIVE

Blessed are all Thy saints, my God and King, who have travelled over the tempestuous sea of mortality, and have at last made the desired port of peace a felicity. Oh, cast a gracious eye upon us who are still on our dangerous voyage. Remember and succour us in our distress, and think on them that lie exposed to the rough storms of troubles and temptations. Strengthen our weakness, that we may do valiantly in this spiritual war; help us against our own negligence and cowardice, and defend us from the treachery of our unfaithful hearts. We are exceeding frail, and indisposed to every virtuous and gallant undertaking. Grant, O Lord, that we may bring our vessel safe to shore, unto our desired haven.

SAINT AUGUSTINE

DAY SIX

Part of prayer is trusting your instincts and spending time with those who also trust your instincts.

DAY SEVEN

Courage, *mon amie,* now is the time to say to yourself, "I will go by what I have seen in calmer moments, with my eyes open. I will take the risk of blind trust." And let your prayer be very simple and not analytic. "O Lord, Thou knowest" is often enough.

MOTHER STUART

Week Forty

DAY ONE

And in the sixth month the angel Gabriel was sent from God unto a city of Galilee, named Nazareth, to a virgin espoused to a man whose name was Joseph, of the house of David; and the virgin's name was Mary. And the angel came in unto her, and said, Hail, thou that art highly favoured, the Lord is with thee: blessed art thou among women.

LUKE 1:26–28

Turn, then, most gracious Advocate, your eyes of
  mercy toward us.
And after this our exile show unto us the blessed
  Fruit of your womb, Jesus.
O clement, O loving, O sweet Virgin Mary.

SALVE REGINA

⁓

DAY TWO

Prayer to the Blessed Virgin

O, most beautiful flower of Mount Carmel, fruitful wine, splendor of heaven, Blessed Mother of the Son of God, Immaculate Virgin, assist me in my necessity. O Star of the Sea, help me and show me here you are my mother. O Holy Mary Mother of God, Queen of heaven and earth, I humbly beseech you from the bottom of my heart to secure me in my necessity. (Make request.)

Say three times:

There are none that can withstand your power. O Mary, conceived without sin, pray for us who have recourse to you.

Say three times:

O Holy Mary, I place this cause in your hands.

⁓

DAY THREE

Mary to Elizabeth:
"My heart is overflowing with praise of my Lord,
my soul is full of joy in God my Saviour.
For he has deigned to notice me, his humble servant
and all generations to come
will call me the happiest of women!

The One who can do all things
has done great things for me —
oh, holy is his Name!
Truly, his mercy rests on those who fear him
in every generation.
He has shown the strength of his arm,
he has swept away the high and mighty.
He has set kings down from their thrones
and lifted up the humble.
He has satisfied the hungry with good things
and sent the rich away with empty hands.
Yes, he has helped Israel, his child:
he has remembered the mercy
that he promised to our forefathers,
to Abraham and his sons for evermore!"

LUKE 1:46–55 The New Testament in Modern
English, J.B. Phillips

⁓

DAY FOUR

Hail, holy Queen, Mother of Mercy, our life, our
sweetness and our hope.
To you do we cry, poor banished children of Eve.
To you do we send up our sighs, mourning and
weeping in this valley of tears.
Turn, then, most gracious Advocate, your eyes of
mercy toward us.

And after this our exile show unto us the blessed
Fruit of your womb, Jesus.
O clement, O loving, O sweet Virgin Mary.

SALVE REGINA

DAY FIVE

And when he was twelve years old, they went up to
Jerusalem after the custom of the feast. And when
they had fulfilled the days, as they returned, the child
Jesus tarried behind in Jerusalem; and Joseph and
his mother knew not of it. . . . And it came to pass,
that after three days they found him in the temple,
sitting in the midst of the doctors, both hearing them
and asking them questions. And all that heard him
were astonished at his understanding and answers.
And when they saw him, they were amazed: and his
mother said unto him, Son, why hast thou thus dealt
with us? behold, thy father and I have sought thee
sorrowing. And he said unto them How is it that ye
sought me? wist ye not that I must be about my
Father's business? And they understood not the saying which he spake unto them.

LUKE 2:42–43, 46–50

DAY SIX

And the third day there was a marriage in Cana of Galilee; and the mother of Jesus was there. . . . And when they wanted wine, the mother of Jesus saith unto him, They have no wine. Jesus saith unto her, Woman, what have I to do with thee? Mine hour is not yet come. His mother saith unto the servants, Whatsoever he saith unto you, do it.

JOHN 2:1, 3–5

DAY SEVEN

Now there stood by the cross of Jesus his mother, and his mother's sister, Mary the wife of Cleophas, and Mary Magdalene.

JOHN 19:25

Week
Forty-one

Day One

Hannah is the first person in Judeo-Christian history recorded to have prayed silently. Deborah's vo-
calization of her personal and national prayer is
among the oldest biblical documents. The mother of
Jesus repeats parts of the prayers of Hannah and
Deborah — her sisters-through-time. Prayer is not
confined to any one gender or any one time.

Day Two

Hear O daughter, consider, and incline your ear;
forget your people, and your father's house, and the
king will desire your beauty. . . .

PSALM 45:10–11

Day Three

What if I am a woman; is not the God of ancient
times the God of these modern days? Did he not

raise up Deborah, to be a mother, and a judge to Israel? Did not Queen Esther save the lives of the Jews? And Mary Magdalene first declare the resurrection of Christ from the dead? Come, said the woman of Samaria, and see a man that hath told me all the things I ever did, is not this the Christ?

A belief, however, that the Deity more readily communicates himself to women, has at one time or other, prevailed in every quarter of the earth; not only among the Germans and the Britons, but all the people of Scandinavia were possessed of it. Among the Greeks, women delivered the Oracles; the respect the Romans paid to the Sibyls, is well known. The predictions of the Egyptian women obtained much credit at Rome, even under Emperors. And, in the most barbarous of nations, all things that have the appearance of being supernatural, the mysteries of religion, the secrets of physic and the rites of magic, were in the possession of women.

Why cannot a religious spirit animate us now?

MRS. MARIA W. STEWART, *Spiritual Narratives*

⁓

DAY FOUR

And it came to pass afterward, that he went throughout every city and village, preaching and showing the glad tidings of the kingdom of God: and the twelve were with him, and certain women, which had been healed of evil spirits and infirmities, Mary called Magdalene, out of whom went seven devils, and Joanna the wife of Chuza Herod's steward, and Susanna, and many others, which ministered unto him of their substance.

LUKE 8:1–3

DAY FIVE

When a person finds a new way to serve God, carry it around with you secretly for nine months as though pregnant with it.

R. YEHUDAH TZVI

DAY SIX

Do I have as much respect for other women as I want God to have for me?

If I wrote a prayer for all women what would it be?

DAY SEVEN

I have no greater joy than to hear that my children walk in truth.

3 JOHN 1:4

Week
Forty-two

DAY ONE

There are many forms of religious belief and practice. Much as one might want to believe that all religions are really one, the fact of the matter is that people believe in and practice religion in all their historicity and context, just as they speak real languages and not some artificial tongue like Esperanto.

DAY TWO

Prayer is the language of relation between God and the individual; the form the prayer takes is as individual as the person praying it.

DAY THREE

O Eternal and most gracious God, who thou beest ever infinite, yet enlargest thyself by the number of our prayers, and takest our often petitions to thee to be an addition to thy glory and thy greatness, as ever upon all occasions, so now, my God, I come to thy majesty with two prayers, two supplications. I have meditated upon the jealousy which thou hast of thine own honour, nearer to the nature of a scorn to thee, than to see thy pardon, and receive the seals of reconciliation to thee, and to return to that sin for which I needed and had thy pardon before. Know that this comes too near to making thy holy ordinances, thy word, thy sacraments, thy seals, thy grace, instruments of my spiritual fornications. Since therefore thy correction hath brought me to such a participation of thyself (thyself O my God, cannot be parted), to such an entire possession of thee, as that I durst deliver myself over to thee this minute, if this minute thou wouldst accept my dissolution, preserve me, O my God, the God of constancy and perserverance, in this state, from all relapses into those sins which have induced thy former judgements upon me. But because, by too lamentable experience, I know how slippery my customs of sin have made my ways of sin, I presume to add this petition too, that if my infirmity overtake me, thou forsake me not. Say to my soul, My son, thou hast sinned, do so no more; but say also, that though I do, thy spirit of remorse and compunction shall never depart from me. Thy holy apostle, St. Paul, was shipwrecked thrice, and yet still saved. Though the rocks and the sands, the heights and the shallows, the prosperity and the adversity of this world, do diversly threaten me, though mine own leaks endanger me, yet, O God, let me never put myself aboard with Hymenaeus, nor make shipwreck of faith and a good conscience, and then thy long-lived, thy everlasting mercy, will visit me, though that which I most earnestly pray against, should fall upon me, a relapse into those sins which I have truly repented, and thou hast fully pardoned.

JOHN DONNE

DAY FOUR

To understand gratitude, I've been collecting examples of people who thank God before there is any evidence to be thankful for. Singers, dancers, actors, athletes, saints, prophets, all laborers in the varied fields of human life thank God before there is evidence. Clipping newspaper stories, magazine articles, and pamphlets with these snippets of gratitude from around the earth is, in itself, a simple form of gratitude.

SARAH SMYTH

DAY FIVE

Saints of God, Praise and Glory to the Lord for He has allowed us one more day to praise His Holy name. Bless the Lord, O my soul. And all that is within me, Praise His Holy Name. Welcome to: "Prayer, A Holy Occupation." Prayer. We are all called to pray. It is the means by which we talk to our Heavenly Father. It is the means by which we bring the Power of the Holy Ghost into a situation, and change it totally, giving Glory to God by it. Prayer. It does avail much, when it is used correctly. Prayer is a holy call, and we as the Priesthood of God, need to pray. For we live in a wicked world, and there is much need for Intercession. Many need the help of God in their lives, but only through prayer can they obtain it. Prayer is essential to the establishing of the Kingdom of God here on earth. No prayer, no Kingdom, Glory, Power, Rule. So prayer is important.

EDWIN CLYMER

DAY SIX

Cause us, our Father, to lie down in peace, and rise up again to enjoy life. Spread over us the covering of Your peace, guide us with Your good counsel and save us for the sake of Your name. Be a shield about us, turning away every enemy, disease, violence, hunger and sorrow. Shelter us in the shadow of Your wings, for You are a God who guards and protects us, a ruler of mercy and compassion. Guard us when we go out and when we come in, to enjoy life and peace both now and forever, and spread over us the shelter of Your peace. Blessed are You, Lord, who spreads the shelter of peace over us, over His people, Israel, and over all the world.

SIDDUR SIM SHALOM

⁓

DAY SEVEN

Pray without ceasing.

1 THESSALONIANS 5:17

Week
Forty-three

DAY ONE

What kind of prayers are you looking for? Love prayers, forgiveness prayers, win-win not-playing-a-game-prayers? The prayers one looks for tells one what is dearest to one's heart, what one is most absorbed with. Requests for prayers are litmus tests of our consciousness.

Ask yourself, what kind of prayers am I looking for?

DAY TWO

Likewise the Spirit also helpeth our infirmities: for we know not what we should pray for as we ought: but the Spirit itself maketh intercession for us with groanings which cannot be uttered.

ROMANS 8:26

DAY THREE

Where my prayers used to be filled with the child-hood "Gimmes" and very little "thank-you-for-the-nice-present," I now rarely pray for myself and then it is usually in conjunction with another person. Instead, I focus my mental and oral petitions in the form of thanksgiving for others and requests for their needs. It is amazing what I receive in response to this method of prayer. I also have a second form of prayer which I did not practice until a couple of years ago. This is Quietude. Some call it meditation, others contemplation. Quietude is different in that I do not focus in on any thing or being upon which to meditate or contemplate. I remain quiet and let God do whatever talking there is to be done and whatever focal points are to be of importance during this prayer time. Sometimes my periods of Quietude become so intense that I lose sense of "being in church" or "being before my altar in my apartment." That is, I am overcome by a sensation that enfolds me, for want of a better description, and "disassociates" me from the surroundings in which I physically am.

ROBERT CARVER

DAY FOUR

Love prayers recognize that we love God because God first loved us.

Write a love prayer that begins with God's love for you.

DAY FIVE

And I said unto the man who stood at the gate of the year, "Give me a little light that I may tread safely into the unknown."

And he replied, "Go out into the darkness and put your hand in the Hand of God. That shall be to you better than light and safer than a known way."

So I went forth, and finding the Hand of God, went gladly into the night. And he led me towards the hills and the breaking of day in the lone East.

M. LOUISE HASKINS

DAY SIX

All prayer is win-win prayer. If nothing else we are healed of the notion that we cannot talk directly with God. Self-reliant, trusting prayers are sure winners.

DAY SEVEN

The Spirit prays for us and with us.

Day One

The easy part of prayer is to be sorry. The hard part is changing behaviour.

Day Two

Forgetting your sins is a proof of having been cleansed of them.

MADAME GUYON

Day Three

Because I knew not when my life was good,
And when there was a light upon my path,
And turned my soul perversely to the dark,
    O Lord, I do repent.

Because I held upon my selfish road,
And left my brothers wounded by the way,

And called ambition duty, and pressed on,
   O Lord, I do repent.

Because I spent the strength Thou gavest me
In struggle which Thou never didst ordain,
And have but dregs of life to offer Thee,
   O Lord, I do repent.

Because I was impatient, would not wait,
But thrust my impious hands across Thy threads
And marred the pattern drawn out for my life,
   O Lord, I do repent.

Because Thou hast borne with me all the time,
Hast smitten me with love until I weep,
Hast called me as a mother calls her child,
   O Lord, I do repent.

SARAH WILLIAMS

DAY FOUR

The highest and most profitable reading is the true knowledge and consideration of ourselves.

THOMAS À KEMPIS

Let us look to our own consciences as we do to our own hands, to see if they be dirty.

FLORENCE NIGHTINGALE

DAY FIVE

Holy Fire

Fire burning bright
Steal away the night
From my dark and lonely soul.
Cleanse my soul, O Fire,
'Til there is but one desire —
My brightly shining goal.
Now burn a path for me
Through the dark and lonely sea
That seethes within my mind.
Fire burning bright
You lead me with your Light
And with each step I find
I come closer to my goal;
    Fulfilling my desire
My dark and lonely soul
Will be one with holy Fire.

KENDRA L. SWOPE

DAY SIX

I admit I am sorry about:

I am doing better. Now.

~~~

DAY SEVEN

Direct us, O Lord, in all our doings with thy most gracious favour, and further us with your continual help; that in all our works begun, continued, and ended in thee, we may glorify your holy Name, and finally, by thy mercy, obtain everlasting life; through Jesus Christ our Lord. Amen.

The Book of Common Prayer (1928)
(Prayer for Guidance)

Week
Forty-five

DAY ONE

O all ye green things upon the earth, bless ye the Lord; praise him and magnify him for ever.

The Book of Common Prayer
(Benedicite, omnia opera Domini)

Most gracious God, by whose knowledge the depths are broken up, and the clouds drop down dew; We yield thee unfeigned thanks and praise for the return of seed-time and harvest, for the increase of the ground and the gathering in of fruits thereof, and for all the other blessings of thy merciful providence bestowed upon this nation and people. And, we beseech thee, give us a just sense of these great mercies; such as may appear in our lives by an humble, holy, and obedient walking before thee all our days. . . .

The Book of Common Prayer (1928)
(from Prayers and Thanksgiving)

Day Two

No longer forward or behind
I look in hope or fear
But grateful take the good I find
the best is now and here.

JOHN GREENLEAF WHITTIER

Day Three

Blessed are the poor in spirit: for theirs is the kingdom of heaven.

Blessed are they that mourn: for they shall be comforted.

Blessed are the meek: for they shall inherit the earth.

Blessed are they which do hunger and thirst after righteousness: for they shall be filled.

Blessed are the merciful: for they shall obtain mercy.

Blessed are the pure in heart: for they shall see God.

Blessed are the peacemakers: for they shall be called the children of God.

Blessed are they which are persecuted for righteousness' sake: for theirs is the kingdom of heaven.

Blessed are ye, when men shall revile you, and persecute you, and shall say all manner of evil against you falsely, for my sake.

JESUS. The Beatitudes. MATTHEW 5:3–11

DAY FOUR

Is there someone I can think of who doesn't like me? Someone saying false things about me? Do I feel blessed by this person and the falsities? Why not?

DAY FIVE

In my distress I called upon the Lord, and cried unto my God: he heard my voice out of his temple, and my cry came before him, even unto his ears.

PSALM 18:6

DAY SIX

Dear Lord, before thy throne,
    Behold thy handmaid fall;
Wilt thou not hear the secret groan,
    And listen when I call?

Oppress'd to thee I fly;
   Thy promised help afford;
No other refuge is there nigh
   But thine, Almighty Lord.

Now, in my low estate,
   Do thou remember me;
One smile my fear shall dissipate,
   And make the darkness flee.

Stretch out thy powerful arm,
   On thee my soul shall rest;
Speak, Lord, and sweet will be the calm
   Within my anxious breast.

The Mother's Hymn Book

DAY SEVEN

And the Lord spake unto Moses, saying, Speak unto
the whole Israelite community and say unto them,
Ye shall be holy: for I the Lord your God am holy.

LEVITICUS 19:1–2.
Tanakh: The Holy Scriptures

Week
Forty-six

DAY ONE

How can we make sure that our desire, our hunger for Good doesn't just disappear into some eternal ether but does fulfill its purpose?

One way to think about God is as unchangeable. For right reasoning in prayer, God is All; ever present.

DAY TWO

If you think God was here but left the earth, then you may have a hard time reaching God. You would no more dial the old telephone number of someone you knew had moved and changed numbers than you should try to "dial" a God that you don't think lives here anymore.

DAY THREE

Catherine called me from Sweden one night and said that she just had to have that chocolate-chip cookie recipe off the back of the yellow package that contained the chips. She had the chips, but no recipe. It was cookie day the next morning at her daughter's school, and she knew that the other mothers had already ordered cookies made at bakeries, had staff help make cookies in their kitchens — there was some talk that the Queen herself was sending over cookies. In this situation home-made Toll House chocolate-chip cookies were the only answer.

I hung up from the call, walked round the corner, bought a package of the chips in the yellow wrapper and, emptying out the chips, faxed the recipe from the back of the package to Sweden. And that's when it dawned on me that the fax is a symbol of God's immediacy. As the information goes into the fax machine it is simultaneously coming out in a specific location in another part of the world. As we pray, the information is simultaneously received. Because if technology can do it, so can God.

The cookies were a big hit.

DAY FOUR

Sometimes we are afraid to leave our traditional the-
ologies or our pastors or our churches or our gurus.
But if the portable phone is an indication of anything,
it is a hint that no matter where we are we are reach-
able and can send messages. Portable phones are
reminders of prayers. There are no strings attached.

DAY FIVE

Make a list of places you think God cannot reach.

Make a list of places you think God can reach.

Compare the length of the lists.

~

DAY SIX

What technology frightens you?

What technology can you translate into spiritual ideas, God's ideas?

~

DAY SEVEN

And it shall come to pass, that before they call, I will answer; and while they are yet speaking, I will hear.

ISAIAH 65:24

Week
Forty-seven

DAY ONE

Prayer is the language of Spirit. Its echoes are in the language of that dimension of spiritual sense that each man, woman and child innately owns.

DAY TWO

Live as the lotus, my child, rise above the muddy
    pond.
Let your blossom be full in the sun,
allow the growth to go beyond.
Your brilliance will be stunning,
all will sense your clarity.
To be in this world but not of it is truly a rarity.
Walk with light feet, my dear,
your shoulders will be strong
Follow one step at a time, though the road may be
    long.
One breath is all this moment brings,
your inspiration ever near

Inhale the light that is with you now
allow it to dispel all fear.
There is a joy within, that is all you need to know.
It is with you for eternity, everywhere you go.
Do not despair or be pulled under, the truth of
    your being
is in the flower.
Trust and faith are yours to have
Believe in this given power.
Simplicity and purpose blend in you,
for life is the connection.
You are a gift to life and it a gift to you,
and there lies the perfection.
Touch on your eternal Soul, abandon yourself to
    its glory.
Make each day a biography, you write your own
    story.
The Creator planted your seed here, surrender to
    your being
With patience and caring, you will soon be seeing.
As you bloom into service, you find your bliss
Your flowership keeps on going
Rest in your beauty, while you float on the stream
Follow your current and flow with the knowing.

JODY TERRY

DAY THREE

A translation of the mundane into an approximation of the sacred is an element of prayer.

Until the day that a friend said to me: "I wash the windows because I love the view," I used to loathe washing the windows. Since that day it has become easier — though not easy — to understand the value of cleansing the five senses and working on establishing a department of spiritual perception in my life. When I take out the garbage I am reminded that I am cleaning out that which is of no value to me. When I sweep I am reminded of cleaning the dust and cobwebs out of my heart.

DAY FOUR

What do I believe? Do I believe the picture my eyes see? Or do I believe what spiritual sense tells me? Today is a fine day to practice spiritual sight. All day.

DAY FIVE

Dear Creator: Show me what you see. Point me full face to a clear view of your Creation.

DAY SIX

The first glimpse of spiritual Creation I have today is of:

The last glimpse is:

DAY SEVEN

Praised are you, Lord our God, King of the Universe, for granting us life; for sustaining us, and for keeping us this day.

Kol Nidre

Week
Forty-eight

Day One

It takes a certain humility to recognize that we are blessed by the prayers of others, even when we do not understand how they work, or even when we have not prayed ourselves.

Day Two

One day recently I was talking about my success, and probably bragging a little bit. And my mother put her hand on my arm, and she said, "Debra, you're successful because I pray for you all the time." And I paused, and I thought, "that probably *is* the reason."

DEBRA BENSON

Day Three

"Most people have had occurrences which might be termed miracles in their own families," wrote William Randolph Hearst in his syndicated column, "In the News," in June 1941. "Your columnist witnessed such a spiritual translation, such an entirely unmaterial healing, such a miraculous rescue of his own son from the very jaws of death." In his column, Hearst recounted the story of a son born with a closed pylorus, the sphincter that connects the stomach with the bowel. This condition made it impossible for the child to retain even a teaspoonful of milk, and without such nourishment, he lost weight, grew alarmingly weak, and hovered near death. The doctors who had been summoned recommended surgery, but they had no confidence that the baby had the strength to survive the operation that might repair his condition.

One evening, during this critical period, a friend of the Hearst family brought a Christian Science practitioner to their home. "Your columnist is not a Christian Scientist," Hearst reported, "but he turned in desperation to this gleam of hope." That night, the practitioner prayed over the child and by morning he was able to take some milk, retain it and begin his recovery. That child, Hearst reported in 1941, was now six feet tall and ran a newspaper "considerably better than his father can."

When he was asked why he never became a Christian Scientist himself, Hearst said that it wasn't as easy for him to change his thinking as it would be for a child. "You know, folks," he explained, "children are the best patients for spiritual healing. . . . [T]hey have no preconceived erroneous convictions — no false beliefs that have to be overcome before the truth can enter their consciousness."

William Randolph Hearst, Jr. (who had been the baby in question) corroborated that this was the way he had always heard the story from his father and mother. The only correction he would have made in the elder Hearst's somewhat florid account was, he remarked, one not of fact but of judgement. "I'm afraid," He wrote wryly, "that neither Pop nor I ever knew the day when I could run a newspaper better than he."

ROBERT PEEL, *Spiritual Healing in a Scientific Age*

DAY FOUR

R. Mendel once commented on the verse "God heard the voice of the lad" (Genesis 21:17) and explained that nothing in the preceding verses had indicated that Ishmael cried out. "No," he explained. "It was a soundless cry and God heard it."

DAY FIVE

I come in the little things,
Saith the Lord;

Yea! on the glancing wings
Of eager birds, the softly pattering feet
Of furred and gentle beasts, I come to meet
Your hard and wayward heart. In brown bright
   eyes
That peep from out the brake, I stand confest.
On every nest
Where feathery Patience in content to brood,
And leaves her pleasure for the high emprise
Of motherhood —
There doth my Godhead rest.

EVELYN UNDERHILL

DAY SIX

Can a woman forget the baby at her breast and have no compassion on the child she has borne? Though she may forget, I will not forget you!

ISAIAH 49:15
New International Version

DAY SEVEN

Mother of the world,
to you we sing
praise and adoration

for life's abundance
and grace.
You provide for our needs
with the bounty of your womb.
You bless us with the touch of your breath
upon our souls.
You caress us with your love
in our hearts.
Praise and thanksgiving
to you we raise,
with joyful hearts
and grateful praise.
Amen.

VIENNA COBB ANDERSON

Week
Forty-nine

Day One

The aim of the human mind to understand and analyze itself is called psychology. The human mind's endeavor to record and interpret the past and to gain a more clearly defined analysis of the present and future is history. Physics is the attempt to systematize the physical environment, and philosophy to see the underlying pattern and relationship of the psyche to its body.

Prayer unifies all aims, attempts, interpretations and patterns.

Day Two

Prayer helps shed the skin of a private, personal, fallible, limited, brain-centered intellect — as a snake sheds its skin.

In prayer we see spiritual reality, not merely a glimpse of a particular way to behave on Planet Earth so that we will find ourselves in some heaven after death.

DAY THREE

We are made in the very image of God.

SIMONE WEIL

DAY FOUR

Prayer works. Even those who know that prayer works remind themselves regularly that it does. Prayer changes things. We do not have to be ashamed, however, that we need to remind ourselves daily that it does.

DAY FIVE

When trouble knocks at the door of my mind, I cannot fight it alone. I must call on the strength of God. It takes a passion to cure a passion. Only the mind and will reborn in the power of God will know the amazing freedom of absolute purity.

KENASTON TWITCHELL

DAY SIX

Audible prayers, no matter how time honored and gorgeous, if spoken with an empty heart do not do the work of spiritual understanding. But if we feel the hope and love in a prayer, then all whom we think of are blessed and better. We have met our friends and family in love and not just in words.

Day Seven

Commit your ways to the Lord and He will bring it to pass.

PSALM 37:5

Commit thy works unto the Lord, and thy thoughts shall be established.

PROVERBS 16:3

Week Fifty

Day One

And there was evening and there was morning — the sixth day. The heavens and the earth, and all they contain, were completed. On the seventh day God completed the work which He had been doing; He ceased on the seventh day from all the work which He had done.

Then God blessed the seventh day and called it holy, because on it He ceased from all His work of Creation.

Genesis 1:31, 2:1–3
Siddur Sim Shalom

Day Two

Praised are You, Lord our God, King of the universe, who makes us holy through doing His commands, and delights in us. Willingly and with love He gives His holy Sabbath to inherit, for it recalls the act of creation. This is the first day of holy gatherings, a reminder of the exodus from Egypt. Thus you have chosen us, endowing us with holiness, from among all peoples by granting us Your holy Shabbat lovingly and gladly. Praised are You, Lord, who hallows Shabbat.

Blessing for the Sabbath
SIDDUR SIM SHALOM

DAY THREE

Take this day to plan ahead for your day of rest. Make it a true day of rest. How will you protect your time on the day of rest?

DAY FOUR

We celebrate Creation.
We celebrate the sacredness of time.

Struggle and dissonance are forgotten;
we are embraced by peace and wholeness.

The Gift of Shabbat
SIDDUR SIM SHALOM

DAY FIVE

Eternity utters a day.

DAY SIX

And it shall come to pass in the last days, that the mountain of the Lord's house shall be established in the top of the mountains, and shall be exalted above the hills; and all nations shall flow into it. And many people will go and say, Come ye, and let us go up to the mountain of the Lord, to the house of the God of Jacob. . . .

ISAIAH 2:2–3

DAY SEVEN

A day of rest.

Week
Fifty-one

DAY ONE

Praying for those in authority is a timeless tradition and, for many, a mandate. Members of many faiths are enjoined to pray daily for the country's leader. Praying for a president or those in authority may seem to some a natural thing to do. Others may think it slavish and beside the point, or hypocritical, to pray for someone you neither care nor voted for.

Prayer for those people you *don't* like is one of the best ways to learn the effectiveness of prayer. It seems simply impossible to pray for someone in authority and not get a better sense of who they are, what their burden is and how difficult their temptations are to face. Prayer brings compassion to the one who prays. Praying for one in authority can also open one's own mind to the possibilities for expanded responsibility and service.

DAY TWO

Hearken unto me, my people; and give ear unto me, O my nation. . . .

ISAIAH 51:4

DAY THREE

Creating a prayer for the leader of a country requires thought.

What kind of prayer could you, in good conscience, pray for the leader of the nation?

DAY FOUR

May the person who is going to live in this house have many children, may he be rich, may he be honest to people and good to the poor; may he not suffer from disease or any other kind of trouble; may he be safe all these years.

KENYAN BLESSING

DAY FIVE

. . . watch and pray. . . .

MARK 13:33b

DAY SIX

And David said, . . . Destroy him not; for who can stretch forth his hand against the Lord's anointed, and be guiltless? . . . The Lord forbid that I should stretch forth my hand against the Lord's anointed. . . .

1 SAMUEL 26:9, 11

DAY SEVEN

The test of all prayer is: do we love our neighbor better for the asking?

MARY BAKER EDDY, *Science and Health with Key to the Scriptures*

Week
❧ Fifty-two ❧

Day One

Make it a policy to never stay where you are not welcomed. This gives you fewer things to pray about.

⌒

Day Two

Let thy work appear unto thy servants, and thy glory unto their children.

PSALM 90:16

⌒

Day Three

As I sit here and reflect on the concluding of this past year, I have realized that many things have happened to me throughout the year. For example, my job of ten years was eliminated, forcing me to rethink and establish a new career; my boyfriend and I made up after a six-month split, and then recently split again — for good this time, I think; my mom was diagnosed with breast cancer, but then made an excellent recovery. My point is this: there have been many learning experiences and many times where I have put my complete faith and trust in God and He has never let me down. I am thankful for His gift of love at the times when it seemed to me that was all I had going for me.

Last year was a tough year for me — a year of sacrifice. I feel that God was testing me, and with his strength and my faith in Him leading me in my decision making for next year, I know that this upcoming year will be the best ever! Do any of you feel that you have experienced the same "test" this year? Are you as optimistic about the year coming up as I am? With God's help and love I know I can achieve great things in his name. And keeping this in mind, I would like to wish you all a very Happy New Year!

RoseAnn, Prodigy Religion On-line

DAY FOUR

Open thou mine eyes, that I may behold wondrous things out of thy law.

PSALM 119:18

DAY FIVE

I make a commitment to myself to pray daily.

I commit to cultivate the practice of prayer.

If I have a problem I will get support for my prayer from someone with experience if the problem sticks around.

I rejoice in being creative about prayer.

I resolve to base my prayers on the All Good and Ever-Presence of Love.

I pray for wisdom.

I pray.

DAY SIX

Because thou hast made the Lord, which is my refuge, even the most High, thy habitation; there shall no evil befall thee, neither shall any plague come nigh thy dwelling. For he shall give his angels charge over thee, to keep thee in all thy ways.

PSALM 91:9–11

DAY SEVEN

Remind yourself of what you already know of prayer. Prayer is the language of Love. And you speak the language.

Appendix
❧ Spiritual Signposts: ❧

VERSES OF COMFORT
INSPIRATION AND DIRECTION FROM THE BIBLE

Where do you go in the Bible when you — this minute — need inspiration, comfort, or an answer to a specific pressing problem? If the Bible were a collection of formulas, everyone would look into its pages on a regular basis. It would all be so simple. Just turn to chapter so-and-so, verse so-and-so and everything will be okay.

But the Bible is not a compilation of formulas. Any formula list of places to go could rob you of the inspiration, comfort or answer that is specifically right for you.

Just imagine. You have a pressing, overwhelming problem. You can hardly breathe. You need help, and you need it now.

Say, for example, that you are the sole support of a family, and you have just been laid off. Your employer says there are cut backs and you'll have to go. Or say that your husband or wife has left you, and you haven't the foggiest idea what to do. Or that your parents have kicked you out of the house.

Is there one verse that will get your job, your husband or wife, or your parental roof back?

Or are there countless places in the Bible that will give you back your breath, reestablish your poise, lead you in the direction you need to go to find another job or a secure and in-control life? Is there a verse that will find work for someone else in your family or open the door for someone to send you a huge amount of money? Is God leading you someplace terrific, where the whole burden won't be on you? Where you will be loved and understood as never before?

Keep going. There is no one answer for everyone. But whatever you need to give you manna or your daily bread for today, whatever inspiration or support or guidance you need may be found.

And take heart. Just one verse can apply to many situations. One example can be found in these words from Psalm 139:

O Lord, thou hast searched me, and known me. Thou knowest my downsitting and mine uprising, thou understandest my thought afar off. . . . Whither shall I go from thy spirit? or whither shall I flee from thy presence? If I ascend up into heaven, thou are there: if I make my bed in hell, behold, thou art there. If I take the wings of the morning, and dwell in the uttermost parts of the sea; even there shall thy hand lead me, and thy right hand shall hold me.

These words could be a great comfort to anyone in any situation, even in the worst of all moments —

the death of a child, any loved one. They say, in those horrific moments of unbelievable pain, that that child or loved one is going nowhere that God's hand is not holding theirs. The entire psalm is an absolute statement of the all-encompassing love, guidance and care of the Creator.

These words may be helpful in finding a job or a new home. But those who read them in the darkest hour of grief may see in them a provision not just for him- or herself but for the one who has left.

On that note let's look at some ways you can find particular verses of inspiration, direction and comfort in the Bible.

- You can open the Bible anywhere and begin reading. That alone may provide an answer.
- You can use a Bible concordance to look up a word or phrase that comes to your mind.
- You can follow the leadings of your own thought —go to another word, another place if you are led.

The Bible itself says that you will get what you ask for.

Let's look at just a bit of one book, Isaiah, to see how the Bible speaks to the issues you may confront today in your life.

Worried about not having had children?

Sing, O barren, thou that didst not bear; break forth into singing, and cry aloud, thou that didst not travail with child: for more are the children of the desolate than the children of the married wife, saith the Lord. (Isaiah 54:1)

Lost your husband and find being a widow nearly impossible?

Fear not; for thou shalt not be ashamed: neither be thou confounded; for thou shalt not be put to shame: for thou shalt forget the shame of thy youth, and shalt not remember the reproach of thy widowhood any more. (54:4)

Looking for a husband? Feel alone on earth without one?

[T]hy Maker is thine husband; the Lord of hosts is his name; and thy Redeemer the Holy One of Israel; The God of the whole earth shall he be called. For the Lord hath called thee as a woman forsaken, and grieved in spirit, and a wife of youth, when thou wast refused, saith thy God. (54:5–6)

Or this might be a place to start for a woman who feels she has been abandoned.

For a small moment have I forsaken thee: but with great mercies will I gather thee. In a little wrath I hid my face from thee for a moment; but with everlasting kindness will I have mercy on thee, saith the Lord thy Redeemer. For this is as the waters of Noah unto me: for as I have sworn that the waters of Noah should go no more over the earth; so have I sworn that I would not be wroth with thee, nor rebuke thee. For the mountains shall depart, and the hills be removed; but my kindness shall not depart from thee, neither shall the covenant of my peace be removed, saith the Lord that hath mercy on thee. (54:7–10)

Or this, when you are worried about your children's education or the direction their lives seem to be taking.

And all thy children shall be taught of the Lord, and great shall be the peace of thy children. (54:13)

From another chapter of Isaiah, this might be a prayer for a woman who wants to get involved in what God can do for her.

Awake, awake, put on strength, O arm of the Lord; awake, as in the ancient days, in the generations of old. Art thou not it that hath cut Rahab, and wounded the dragon? Art thou not it which hath dried the sea, the waters of the great deep; that hath made the depths of the sea a way for the ransomed to pass over? Therefore the redeemed of the Lord shall return, and come with singing unto Zion; and everlasting joy shall be upon their head: they shall obtain gladness and joy; and sorrow and mourning shall flee away. (Isaiah 51:9)

Think you can't make something work for you? Or that you can't finish a project?

So shall my word be that goeth forth out of my mouth: it shall not return unto me void, but it shall accomplish that which I please, and it shall prosper in the thing whereto I sent it. (Isaiah 55:11)

Depressed?

For ye shall go out with joy, and be led forth with peace; the mountains and the hills shall break forth before you into singing, and all the trees of the field shall clap their hands. (55:12)

Think your life amounts to nothing?

For as the new heavens and the new earth, which I will make, shall remain before me, saith the Lord, so shall your seed and your name remain. (Isaiah 66:22)

Now, as a reminder of how your needs may vary and how just one Bible verse can apply to many situations, look at this one from Psalms:

Hold up my goings in thy paths, that my footsteps slip not. (Psalm 17:5)

Is this the verse for those going off on a mountain-climbing expedition? Or for someone who is getting older and is losing her balance? Or is it a cry from a woman who wants to be smart and spiritual and is afraid she is about to say "yes" to the wrong man? Is it about support in the endless activity of spiritual creation? Or a prayer for courage? Or none of the above? What it means is established in the context of the Bible. How and when its meaning applies to your life only you can say.

Here are some ideas from the Bible that may speak to your current struggle. They are arranged in the order of the books in the Authorized (King James)

Version of the Bible, but that doesn't mean that you shouldn't go directly to the words that meet your present need.

They are presented without comment. It is up to you to write in this book, the Bible, your notebook or journal how and when these words from the Scriptures apply and speak to you. Whether you find them helpful or annoying, still they speak to need, identity, incest, child abuse, personal debt, the economy, women's rights, male-female relationships, aloneness.

Try it yourself. Apply the words of the Bible to your life situation and its needs today. Remember, each day is different and the biblical God meets your daily needs.

And of every living thing of all flesh, two of every sort shalt thou bring into the ark, to keep them alive with thee, they shall be male and female. (Genesis 6:19)

I am the Lord thy God, which have brought thee out of the land of Egypt, out of the house of bondage. (Exodus 20:2)

The nakedness of thy sister, the daughter of thy father, or daughter of thy mother, whether she be born at home, or born abroad, even their nakedness thou shalt not uncover.

The nakedness of thy son's daughter, or of thy daughter's daughter, even their nakedness thou shalt not uncover: for theirs is thine own nakedness.

The nakedness of thy father's wife's daughter, begotten of thy father, she is thy sister, thou shalt not uncover her nakedness.

Thou shalt not uncover the nakedness of thy father's sister: she is thy father's near kinswoman.

Thou shalt not uncover the nakedness of thy mother's sister: for she is thy mother's near kinswoman.

Thou shalt not uncover the nakedness of thy father's brother, thou shalt not approach to his wife: she is thine aunt.

Thou shalt not uncover the nakedness of thy daughter in law: she is thy son's wife; thou shalt not uncover her nakedness.

Thou shalt not uncover the nakedness of thy brother's wife: it is thy brother's nakedness.

Thou shalt not uncover the nakedness of a woman and her daughter, neither shalt thou take her son's daughter, or her daughter's daughter, to uncover her nakedness; for they are her near kinswomen: it is wickedness.

Neither shalt thou take a wife to her sister, to vex her, to uncover her nakedness, beside the other in her life time.

Also thou shalt not approach unto a woman to uncover her nakedness, as long as she is put apart for her uncleanness.

Moreover thou shalt not lie carnally with thy neighbour's wife to defile thyself with her. (Leviticus 18:9–20)

And yet for all that, when they be in the land of their enemies, I will not cast them away, neither will I abhor them, to destroy them utterly, and to break my covenant with them: for I am the Lord their God. (Leviticus 26:44)

In the year of the jubilee the field shall return unto him of whom it was bought, even to him to whom the possession of the land did belong. (Leviticus 27:24)

And it shall be forgiven all the congregation of the children of Israel, and the stranger that sojourneth among them; seeing all the people were in ignorance. (Numbers 15:26)

God is not a man, that he should lie; neither the son of man, that he should repent: hath he said, and shall he not do it? or hath he spoken, and shall he not make it good? (Numbers 23:19)

And the Lord heard the voice of your words, when ye spake unto me; and the Lord said unto me, I have heard the voice of the words of this people, which they have spoken unto thee: they have well said all that they have spoken. O that there were such an heart in them, that they would fear me, and keep my commandments always, that it might be well with them, and with their children for ever! (Deuteronomy 5:28–29)

Hear, O Israel: The Lord our God is one Lord: And thou shalt love the Lord thy God with all thine heart, and with all thy soul, and with all thy might. And these words, which I command thee this day, shall be in thine heart: And thou shalt teach them diligently unto thy children, and shalt talk of them when thou sittest in thine house, and when thou walkest by the way, and when thou liest down, and when thou risest up. And thou shalt bind them for a sign upon thine hand, and they shall be as frontlets between thine eyes. And thou shalt write them upon the posts of thy house, and on thy gates. (Deuteronomy 6:4–9)

But because the Lord loved you, and because he would keep the oath which he had sworn unto your fathers, hath the Lord brought you out with a mighty hand, and redeemed you out of the house of bondmen, from the hand of Pharaoh king of Egypt. Know therefore that the Lord thy God, he is God, the faithful God, which keepeth covenant and mercy with them that love him and keep his commandments to a thousand generations. . . . (Deuteronomy 7:8–9)

And he will love thee, and bless thee, and multiply thee: he will also bless the fruit of thy womb, and the fruit of thy land, thy corn, and thy wine, and thine oil, the increase of thy kine, and the flocks of thy sheep, in the land which he sware unto thy fathers to give thee. Thou shalt be blessed above all people: there shall not be male or female barren among you, or among your cattle. And the Lord will take away from thee all sickness. . . . (Deuteronomy 7:13–15)

And Joshua saved Rahab the harlot alive, and her father's household, and all that she had; and she dwelleth in Israel even unto this day; because she hid the messengers, which Joshua sent to spy out Jericho. (Joshua 6:25)

Hear, O ye kings; give ear, O ye princes; I, even I, will sing unto the Lord; I will sing praise to the Lord God of Israel. (Judges 5:3)

When ye go, ye shall come unto a people secure, and to a large land: for God hath given it into your hands; a place where there is no want of any thing that is in the earth. (Judges 18:10)

The Lord recompense thy work, and a full reward be given thee of the Lord God of Israel, under whose wings thou art come to trust. (Ruth 2:12)

And now, my daughter, fear not; I will do to thee all that thou requires. . . . (Ruth 3:11)

Talk no more so exceeding proudly; let not arrogancy come out of your mouth: for the Lord is a God of knowledge, and by him actions are weighed. (1 Samuel 2:3)

And David said to Saul, Wherefore hearest thou men's words, saying, Behold, David seeketh thy hurt? Behold, this day thine eyes have seen how that the Lord had delivered thee to day into mine hand in the cave: and some bade me kill thee: but mine eye spared thee; and I said, I will not put forth mine hand against my lord; for he is the Lord's anointed. (1 Samuel 24:1–10)

I have surely built thee an house to dwell in, a settled place for thee to abide in for ever. (1 Kings 8:13)

I beseech thee, O Lord, remember now how I have walked before thee in truth and with a perfect heart, and have done that which is good in thy sight. (2 Kings 20:3)

O Lord, for thy servant's sake, and according to thine own heart, hast thou done all this greatness, in making known all these great things. O Lord, there is none like thee, neither is there any God beside thee, according to all that we have heard with our ears. (1 Chronicles 17:19–20)

Thine, O Lord, is the greatness, and the power, and the glory, and the victory, and the majesty: for all that is in the heaven and in the earth is thine; thine is the kingdom, O Lord, and thou art exalted as head above all. (1 Chronicles 29:11)

. . . Thus saith the Lord unto you, Be not afraid nor dismayed by reason of this great multitude; for the battle is not yours, but God's. (2 Chronicles 20:11)

. . . I am doing a great work, so that I cannot come down: why should the work cease, whilst I leave it, and come down to you? (Nehemiah 6:3)

For how can I endure to see the evil that shall come unto my people? or how can I endure to see the destruction of my kindred? (Esther 8:6)

The Spirit of God hath made me, and the breath of the Almighty hath given me life. (Job 33:4)

Hearken, O daughter, and consider, and incline thine ear; forget also thine own people, and thy father's house; so shall the king greatly desire thy beauty: for he is thy Lord; and worship thou him. The king's daughter is all glorious within: her clothing is of wrought gold. (Psalm 45:10–11, 13)

As a jewel of gold in a swine's snout, so is a fair woman which is without discretion. (Proverbs 11:22)

Let us hear the conclusion of the whole matter: Fear God, and keep his commandments: for this is the whole duty of man. (Ecclesiastes 12:13)

I am my beloved's, and his desire is toward me. (Song of Solomon 7:10)

Many waters cannot quench love, neither can the floods drown it. . . . (Song of Solomon 8:7)

Lift up thine eyes round about, and see: all they gather themselves together, they come to thee: thy sons shall come from far, and thy daughters shall be nursed at thy side. (Isaiah 60:4)

For, behold, I create new heavens and a new earth: and the former shall not be remembered, nor come into mind. (Isaiah 65:17)

For I have heard a voice as of a woman in travail, and the anguish as of her that bringeth forth her first child, the voice of the daughter of Zion, that bewaileth herself, that spreadeth her hands, saying, Woe is me now! for my soul is wearied because of murderers. (Jeremiah 4:31)

Mine eye affecteth mine heart because of all the daughters of my city. (Lamentations 3:51)

What mean ye, that ye use this proverb concerning the land of Israel, saying, The fathers have eaten sour grapes, and the children's teeth are set on edge? As I live, saith the Lord God, ye shall not have occasion any more to use this proverb in Israel. (Ezekiel 18:2–3)

I thought it good to shew the signs and wonders that the high God hath wrought toward me. (Daniel 4:2–3)

And I will betroth thee unto me for ever; yea, I will betroth thee unto me in righteousness, and in judgment, and in lovingkindness, and in mercies. (Hosea 2:19)

Blow the trumpet in Zion, sanctify a fast, call a solemn assembly: gather the people, sanctify the congregation, assemble the elders, gather the children, and those that suck the breasts: let the bridegroom go forth of his chamber, and the bride out of her closet. (Joel 2:15–16)

When my soul fainted within me I remembered the Lord: and my prayer came in unto thee, into thine holy temple. (Jonah 2:7)

Arise and thresh, O daughter of Zion: for I will make thine horn iron, and I will make thy hoofs brass: and thou shalt beat in pieces many people: and I will consecrate their gain unto the Lord, and their substance unto the Lord of the whole earth. . . . Now gather thyself in troops, O daughter of troops. . . . (Micah 4:13, 5:1)

For now I will break his yoke from off thee, and will burst thy bonds in sunder. (Nahum 1:13)

Thou art of purer eyes than to behold evil, and canst not look on iniquity. . . . (Habakkuk 1:13)

Behold, at that time I will undo all that afflict thee: and I will save her that halteth, and gather her that was driven out; and I will get them praise and fame in every land where they have been put to shame. (Zephaniah 3:19)

Thus saith the Lord of hosts, Consider your ways. (Haggai 1:7)

Sing and rejoice, O daughter of Zion: for, lo, I

come, and I will dwell in the midst of thee, saith the Lord. (Zechariah 2:10)

Bring ye all the tithes into the storehouse, that there may be meat in mine house, and prove me now herewith, saith the Lord of hosts, if I will not open you the windows of heaven, and pour you out a blessing, that there shall not be room enough to receive it. (Malachi 3:10)

... Why trouble ye the woman for she hath wrought a good work upon me. (Matthew 26:10)

And he came and took her by the hand, and lifted her up; and immediately the fever left her, and she ministered unto them. (Mark 1:31)

Heaven and earth shall pass away: but my words shall not pass away. (Luke 21:33)

God is a Spirit: and they that worship him must worship him in spirit and in truth. (John 4:24)

And it shall come to pass in the last days, saith God, I will pour out of my Spirit upon all flesh: and your sons and your daughters shall prophesy, and your young men shall see visions, and your old men shall dream dreams: and on my servants and on my handmaidens I will pour out in those days of my Spirit; and they shall prophesy. . . . (Acts 2:17–18)

Be not overcome of evil, but overcome evil with good. (Romans 12:21)

For we know in part, and we prophecy in part. (1 Corinthians 13:9)

Now the Lord is that Spirit: and where the Spirit of the Lord is, there is liberty. (2 Corinthians 3:17)

But if ye be led of the Spirit, ye are not under The law. (Galatians 5:18)

For we wrestle not against flesh and blood, but against principalities, against powers, against the rulers of the darkness of this world, against spiritual wickedness in high places. Wherefore take unto you the whole armour of God. (Ephesians 6:12–13)

Let nothing be done through strife or vainglory; but in lowliness of mind let each esteem other better than themselves. (Philippians 2:3)

Continue in prayer, and watch in the same with thanksgiving; (Colossians 4:2)

For ye are our glory and our joy. (1 Thessalonians 2:20)

Comfort your hearts, and stablish you in every good word and work. (2 Thessalonians 2:17)

For every creature of God is good, and nothing to be refused, if it be received with thanksgiving; (1 Timothy 4:4)

For God hath not given us the spirit of fear; but of power, and of love, and of a sound mind. (2 Timothy 1:7)

For a bishop must be blameless, as the steward of God; not selfwilled, not soon angry, not given to filthy lucre; but a lover of hospitality, a lover of good men, sober, just, holy, temperate. . . . (Titus 1:7–8)

I thank my God, making mention of thee always in my prayers, (Philemon 1:4)

For the word of God is quick, and powerful, and sharper than any two-edged sword, piercing even to the dividing asunder of soul and spirit, and of the joints and marrow, and is a discerner of the thoughts and intents of the heart. (Hebrews 4:12)

Every good gift and every perfect gift is from above, and cometh down from the Father of lights, with whom is no variableness, neither shadow of turning. (James 1:17)

Finally, be ye all of one mind, having compassion one of another, love as brethren, be pitiful, be courteous: (1 Peter 3:8)

Nevertheless we, according to his promise, look for new heavens and a new earth, wherein dwelleth righteousness. (2 Peter 3:13)

This then is the message which we have heard of him, and declare unto you, that God is light, and in him is no darkness at all. (1 John 1:5)

And now I bessech thee, lady, not as though I wrote a new commandment unto thee, but that which we had from the beginning, that we love one another. (2 John 1:5)

I have no greater joy than to hear that my children walk in truth. (3 John 1:4)

Now unto him that is able to keep you from falling, and to present you faultless before the presence of his glory with exceeding joy, To the only wise God our Saviour, be glory and majesty, dominion and power, both now and ever. Amen. (Jude 1:25)

And God shall wipe away all tears from their eyes; and there shall be no more death, neither sorrow, nor crying, neither shall there be any more pain: for the former things are passed away. (Revelation 21:4)

❧ Acknowledgments ❧

While the varieties of prayer experience in this book come from many tongues and hearts through time, the basic sentiments are the same.

Special thanks to Emily Newhall Ennis for lending me the prayer books that sustained her aunt, Milly Fowler, through a lifetime; to Bruce J. Ennis for the prayer book inspired by the thoughts and life of his father, Bruce J. Ennis, Sr.; and to Jon Richards for the prayer books cherished by his family for over the last century and a half,

Thanks always to Helen Hoel Knudson for her shared personal experience, endless hospitality and cheerful support; to Marion Robman for her sustaining interest and support; to Merri-Jim McLaughlin, who over a decade ago suggested keeping an appointment calendar and prayer journal on the same pages; and to Wilmot Reeves, her grandfather-in-law, whose cherished copy of the *International Bible Lessons*, begun in 1884, reminded us of the roots of the tradition of daily prayer in our lives.

Sylvia Friedman. Thank you. Sydny Miner. Thank you. Elizabeth Becker, thank you for praying through this year with me.

Fern Bernstein-Miller, Frederica Daly, Kendra L. Swope, Robert Carver, Jody Terry, Carolyn Maloney, Sharon Lawlor, Ed Vis, Vanessa Cole, Desiree Brassette graciously gave permission to use the prayers they had posted on the Religious Writing topic of the Prodigy Religion Bulletin Boards.

Unless otherwise noted, biblical selections are from the King James version of the Bible.

Permissions (*continued from p. 4*)

University Press. *Miracle of Mindfulness*, by Thich Nhat Hanh, Copyright © 1975, 1976 by Thich Nhat Hanh, reprinted by permission of Beacon Press. *Prayers of Our Hearts: In Word and Action*, by Vienna Cobb Anderson, Copyright © 1991 by Vienna Cobb Anderson, reprinted by permission of The Crossroads Publishing Co., New York. *Spiritual Healing in a Scientific Age*, by Robert Peel, reprinted by permission of A.W. Phinney, Lee Z. Johnson, Executors, Estate of Robert Peel. *Miss Manners Guide to Excruciatingly Correct Behavior*, by Judith Martin, Copyright © 1979, 1980, 1981, 1982 by Judith Martin, reprinted by permission of Simon & Schuster, Inc. *Healing Words: The Power of Prayer and the Practice of Medicine*, by Larry Dossey, M.D., Copyright © 1993 by Larry Dossey, reprinted by permission of HarperCollins Publishers. *Prayers for Meditation*, by Karl Rahner, reprinted by permission of Burns & Oates Limited.